THE RULES OF LEADERSHIP

I0806052

Pearson

At Pearson, we have a simple mission: to help people make more of their lives through learning.

We combine innovative learning technology with trusted content and educational expertise to provide engaging and effective learning experiences that serve people wherever and whenever they are learning.

From classroom to boardroom, our curriculum materials, digital learning tools and testing programmes help to educate millions of people worldwide – more than any other private enterprise.

Every day our work helps learning flourish, and wherever learning flourishes, so do people.

To learn more, please visit us at **www.pearson.com**

THE RULES OF LEADERSHIP

A definitive code for leadership success

RICHARD TEMPLAR

Pearson

Harlow, England • London • New York • Boston • San Francisco • Toronto • Sydney
Dubai • Singapore • Hong Kong • Tokyo • Seoul • Taipei • New Delhi
Cape Town • São Paulo • Mexico City • Madrid • Amsterdam • Munich • Paris • Milan

PEARSON EDUCATION LIMITED
KAO Two
KAO Park
Harlow CM17 9NA
United Kingdom
Tel: +44 (0)1279 623623
Web: www.pearson.com

First edition published 2026 (print and electronic)
© Richard Templar 2026 (print and electronic)

The right of Richard Templar to be identified as author of this work has been asserted by him in accordance with the Copyright, Designs and Patents Act 1988.

The print publication is protected by copyright. Prior to any prohibited reproduction, storage in a retrieval system, distribution or transmission in any form or by any means, electronic, mechanical, recording or otherwise, permission should be obtained from the publisher or, where applicable, a licence permitting restricted copying in the United Kingdom should be obtained from the Copyright Licensing Agency Ltd, Barnard's Inn, 86 Fetter Lane, London EC4A 1EN.

The ePublication is protected by copyright and must not be copied, reproduced, transferred, distributed, leased, licensed or publicly performed or used in any way except as specifically permitted in writing by the publisher, as allowed under the terms and conditions under which it was purchased, or as strictly permitted by applicable copyright law. Any unauthorised distribution or use of this text may be a direct infringement of the author's and the publisher's rights and those responsible may be liable in law accordingly.

All trademarks used herein are the property of their respective owners. The use of any trademark in this text does not vest in the author or publisher any trademark ownership rights in such trademarks, nor does the use of such trademarks imply any affiliation with or endorsement of this book by such owners.

Pearson Education is not responsible for the content of third-party internet sites.

ISBN: 978-1-292-76670-6 (print)
978-1-292-49902-4 (ePub)

British Library Cataloguing-in-Publication Data
A catalogue record for the print edition is available from the British Library

Library of Congress Cataloging-in-Publication Data
A catalog record for the print edition is available from the Library of Congress

10 9 8 7 6 5 4 3 2 1
30 29 28 27 26

Cover design by Nick Redeyoff

Print edition typeset in 11/13pt ITC Berkeley Oldstyle Pro by Straive
Printed in the UK by Bell and Bain Ltd, Glasgow

NOTE THAT ANY PAGE CROSS REFERENCES REFER TO THE PRINT EDITION

Contents

Introduction

What is a good leader? To answer that, you have to understand the difference between leadership and management. Of course there's a big overlap. In business terms, in fact, leaders are a subset of managers: all leaders are managers, but not all managers are leaders.

A manager runs a team or a department or a company in functional terms. They organise, administer, co-ordinate, set objectives and ensure they are met, make decisions, acquire and distribute resources, plan, hire and fire, and solve operational problems.

That sounds like plenty to be getting on with. But a leader does all that and more. A leader is responsible not only for the operation of the team and its function, but also for the motivation, welfare and emotional engagement of the people within it. Managing is about the job you do. Leadership is about the way the people who you manage actually feel.

As a leader, it's down to you to create a positive culture that inspires your team to feel positive about their work, to trust each other, to communicate well, to believe they have a voice, to feel valued, to buy into the culture you've created, and to want to perform well. It's your job to create a vision of what your team or department or organisation can be, and to sell that vision to your people.

Good leaders know that a well-led team will be far more effective. However, this isn't a cynical exercise in driving up productivity. The best leaders are the ones who genuinely buy into the whole culture of working in a motivated and collaborative group of people who can achieve far more together than they can separately.

Of course there are different styles of leadership, and leaders are all individuals with their own personalities and motivations and objectives. But there are common approaches that unite all good leaders, common Rules they all live by. The Rules of Leadership.

The very first book in this series, published back in 2004, was *The Rules of Work*. I followed this with *The Rules of Management*. In many ways, this second book was really about leadership, because all the best managers are leaders at heart. However, there were many Rules of Work that also feed into leadership, because much of it is about who you are, what you believe in, how you work. To be a really great leader, you have to have your own house in order, your own work style sorted. And if you aspire to lead bigger groups and departments and, eventually, perhaps whole organisations, you need to understand how to make that happen. It's not only about constantly improving as a leader, but also about making sure your bosses know how good you are.

So the time felt right to bring together many of the key Rules from across these two books into one volume focused on leadership. Along with a few additional Rules – some inspired by changes in working practices over the last 20-plus years – this volume is entirely focused on those Rules which will guide you to become a great leader, and to make sure that you are positioned to keep moving upwards to ever more challenging and exciting leadership roles.

If you've read any of the other books in this series, you'll know that life as a Rules Player isn't necessarily easy. Exciting, yes. Fun, yes. Challenging, rewarding, satisfying, successful, inspiring – all yes. But easy? No. I can't promise you that. After all, if it was easy, everyone would be a brilliant leader, and I think we all know that's not the case. Then again, leaders need people to follow them, and good followers make the world go round. They're the ones who get the hard work done. So it's up to you to give those good people the great leaders they deserve, so they can feel happy and positive and inspired and valued.

These Rules may be demanding – you'll find some easier than others – but they are all achievable. There's nothing in here that you can't learn if you have the willingness and are ready to put in the work. You've already picked up this book, so I'm guessing you already have that spark – whether you're just starting out on your career, or whether you're already a manager who understands that leadership is another step up, and you're ready to take that step. Either way, the Rules of leadership will transform you from a good manager to a truly great leader.

Richard Templar

How to use the Rules

It can be a bit daunting to read a book with 100 Rules for a happier more successful life. I mean, where do you start? You'll probably find you follow a few of them already, but how can you be expected to learn dozens of new Rules all at once and start putting them all into practice? Don't panic, you don't have to. Remember, you don't have to do anything – you're doing this because you want to. Let's keep it at a manageable level so you go on wanting to.

You can go about this any way you like, but if you want advice, here's what I recommend. Go through the book and pick out three or four Rules that you feel would make a big difference to you, or that jumped out at you when you first read them, or that seem like a good starting point for you. Write them down here:

Just work on these for a couple of weeks until they've become ingrained and you don't have to try so hard with them. They've become a habit. Great stuff, well done. Now you can repeat the exercise with a few more Rules you'd like to tackle next. Write them here:

Excellent. Now you're really making progress. Keep working through the Rules at your own pace – there's no rush. Before long you'll find you're really getting on top of all the Rules that will help you, and more and more of them are becoming ingrained. And voilà! Congratulations – you're a proper Rules Player.

ASSEMBLE YOUR TEAM

In order to be a leader, you first need someone to follow you. Yep, that's your team. When you first start out on your career as a leader, you'll likely be given a team to lead. You may not have much control over who is in it, but at least you can understand who they are and how they fit together, and you can start to shape how the various people in your team work together as a unit.

It won't be long before you get the chance to start tweaking. People leave or move on and need replacing. Or your team is so successful with you as its leader that it needs to grow. You'll have more control over how your team looks. Maybe you even get asked to set up a new team, and can pick the right people from the start.

As you move up the ladder, your teams get bigger, and your control over them increases. And how well those teams perform will be entirely down to you. You pick 'em, you train 'em, you motivate 'em, you lead 'em. The buck stops with you. So these first few Rules are all about making sure you have the right people and the right culture to get the best out of them.

RULE 1

Know what a team is and how it works

So what is a team and how does it operate? If we are going to be successful leaders we have to know the answers to these questions.

A team isn't a collection of people. It is an organisation with its own dynamics, qualities and conventions. Without knowing these things you will flounder. Knowing them, you can work your team to achieve greatness.

In every team there is a variety of people all pushing and shoving in different directions and with unequal force. Some shove louder, if you know what I mean. Others are happy to push from the back. Others don't appear to be doing anything, but you'll need them for ideas.

If you haven't looked at team dynamics before, I urge you to read Meredith Belbin's *Management Teams: Why they succeed or fail*.* (If you have, pass right on to the next Rule.) This is designed for leaders concerned with achieving results by getting the best from their key people. I'll paraphrase what he says, but I do urge you to practise what he preaches.

Belbin says that there are nine team roles – and we all carry out one or more functions of these team roles. Yes, it is fun to identify our own, but it is much more useful to identify your team's and then work with that information.

The nine team roles are the Plant (that's the ideas person), the Resource Investigator, the Co-ordinator, the Shaper, the Monitor Evaluator, the Team Worker, the Implementer, the Completer and

---

* *Management Teams: Why they succeed or fail* by R. Meredith Belbin (Routledge, 3rd edition, 2013)

the Specialist. If you want to know more, you'll have to read the book.

Now you know who you might have in your team. So what exactly is a team and how are you going to make yours more effective? Again, read Belbin and also come to understand that a team is a group where all the members focus on a collective target. A team doesn't pull together well when each individual member focuses on their own target – be that just getting to the end of the day, their own personal progress, how to stitch up the boss (that's you, by the way), using work as a social club, etc.

You'll know you have a team when you hear 'we' and 'us' more often than 'I' and 'me'.

You'll know you have a team when difficult decisions become easy – because someone says, 'It's OK, we're all in this together'.

You'll know you have a team when the team tells you it is a team.

A TEAM DOESN'T PULL TOGETHER WELL WHEN EACH INDIVIDUAL MEMBER FOCUSES ON THEIR OWN TARGET

Hire raw talent

Do you know how many publishers turned down William Golding's *Lord of the Flies*? I've heard several numbers quoted, but the answer is at least a dozen, whoever you ask. And what does that say about the publisher who finally signed up the author? To just about everyone it says he was a whole lot smarter than all the guys who turned the book down.

Every hugely successful leader was once fresh out of school or college, waiting for someone to recognise their talent and offer them a job. They were junior managers looking for promotion, or middle managers hoping it would be them who'd be asked to head up the new project or department or enterprise.

These are the people you want on your team. The raw talent, ready to step up. Never mind about experience – anyone can get that, given time. But you can't fake real talent, brains, energy. When you find someone who has those, offer them the job first and worry about the details later. I'm not talking about mere enthusiasm – sadly lots of untalented people have that – but real ability and an intelligent grasp of the issues they'll be dealing with.

Of course, these talented recruits could eventually outshine you. They could fly up the career ladder and even overtake you. That worries some people. A lot. But it doesn't worry a Rules Player. You see, Rules Players understand that if it says anything about them at all, it will be reflected glory that shines on them. Just like the publisher who offered William Golding his first contract.

Think about it. These people are going to get to the top with or without you. How much better to be the one who had the perception to recognise them, the sense to hire them and the privilege to set them on their upward way.

Once you start putting your own team together, the people in it and their performance says more about you as a leader than anything else does. The better the team, the more impressed people will be with you. Hell, some top leaders will confess to you that their only real talent has been in hiring people who were smarter than them. They may say it self-deferentially, but actually it's really the only skill you need to get to the top. Know who to hire, and then stay out of their way except to give them what they need to do the job. That doesn't make you a bad leader, it makes you a top-class one, because your team will outperform the rest thanks to your talent-spotting skills.

THINK ABOUT IT. THESE PEOPLE ARE GOING TO GET TO THE TOP WITH OR WITHOUT YOU

Be very, very good at finding the right people

You have to be good at finding the right people to fill the right jobs – and then leave them to get on with it. OK, I know this is one rule that requires a certain intuitive touch but I'm sure you know the sort of manager I'm talking about. They seem to surround themselves with capable, competent people and then they just seem to sit back and watch them go for goal. You can do that too. It is a special talent but one you can cultivate. I guess the skill is in both picking the right people *and* letting go – leaving them alone to get on with it. You have to have lots of trust to do that; trust in their ability and trust in your own as well.

You have to have a very clear idea of *who* you are looking for to fill a job as much as *what* you are looking for. For instance, you might need a senior account manager – that is *what* you are looking for. But *who*? Team player? Good all-rounder? Someone able to make decisions on the run? Someone who can plan ahead? Someone who understands your industry's quirks? Someone who speaks fluent spreadsheet? Someone who can work with an over-excitable union?

I'm sure you get the idea. If you have a clear picture of *who* you need as well as *what* you need, you make the transition to being a leader who seems to have an uncanny knack of finding the right people. It's not a knack, of course, but planning, vision, logic and hard work.

I once made the mistake of being totally seduced by a manager's credentials – I was a general manager seeking to employ a manager – and failing to look hard enough at *who* he was rather than *what* he was. Yes, he had the credentials and was very good at his job. But he wasn't a team player and saw everything as a competition, mainly between him and the other managers. Fine in itself, but it didn't work for me or the other managers, who all wanted to pull together. This was one case where I was not good at finding the right person. I had found the wrong person and it took a lot to extricate myself. I had only myself to blame because I hadn't thought sufficiently about who I wanted.

If you're not good at this, or think you could improve, invite somebody you respect to sit in on interviews with you to give you another perspective. Find a mentor or coach to help you work out who you really need.

> **YOU HAVE TO BE GOOD AT FINDING THE RIGHT PEOPLE TO FILL THE RIGHT JOBS – AND THEN LEAVE THEM TO GET ON WITH IT**

If you can't find the right person, don't hire the wrong one

You'd think this would be obvious, wouldn't you? No one's knowingly going to hire the wrong person, surely. Ah, but lots of people do it *un*knowingly. You advertise the job, you get several potentially promising applicants, you hold interviews, you hire the best one. What's wrong with that?

I'll tell you what's wrong with it. You haven't considered the possibility that once you meet them, maybe *none* of them is the right candidate. Of course very often the best applicant will be brilliant, and they'll be a perfect hire. That's great, so long as it doesn't lull you into thinking that's the way it always goes.

The key here is to remember that you're not judging the candidates against each other, so you can rank them and offer the job to whoever comes out on top. You need to measure each candidate independently against the criteria you've set for the job (bearing in mind Rule 3). That's all that matters. You don't want to appoint someone, however impressive, if their strengths are not in the right areas. Lots of impressive people apply for jobs every day, but that doesn't make them right for every post they apply for. They have to be the right match specifically for the role you're trying to fill.

Actually, this can be helpful. I recall one particular interview panel where we had two outstanding internal applicants and initially we really couldn't choose between them. So we went back to the job spec and realised that one of them was clearly a better match for this particular role.

One of the most frequent objections to this particular Rule is that if you don't appoint, you have no one at all doing the job in question. 'Help!' you say, 'We can't function without a marketing director / receptionist / service manager / whatever. We *have* to fill the post!' I still say, no you don't. If you appoint the wrong person, they could still be in the job in five years' time, and still be wrong. You'll have committed yourselves to potentially years of not having a decent marketing director / receptionist / service manager / whatever. How costly will that be?

There's always a better option. What would you do if your marketing manager – or whoever – went on maternity leave? Or was unexpectedly in hospital for three months? Whatever the answer to that question is, do that while you re-advertise the post. You might make a temporary hire, or find other people to cover, or split tasks differently and create an alternative role, or hire two part-timers… you can be as creative as you like so long as, in the longer term, all roles are being done by people who really suit the job.

IF YOU APPOINT THE WRONG PERSON, THEY COULD STILL BE IN THE JOB IN FIVE YEARS' TIME, AND STILL BE WRONG

RULE 5

Ensure people know exactly what is expected of them

It's easy to give someone a job description and a contract and then sit back and expect them to get on with it. Trouble is, it leads to a lot of confused people and wasted time. Better to let them know right from the off what is expected of them.

And what is expected of them? Well, it's a whole lot more than just the job itself. You have to think through every individual role and what *exactly* is expected of that person.

It's vital that people know what part they play in any strategic plan and what is expected of them as a result. It's essential that team members know the values and standards of the team and the company, and what's expected of them in attitude and behaviour (open? honest? imaginative? caring? can do?). It's also about them being clear on emotional requirements, punctuality, working overtime, behaviour towards colleagues, crisis management – everything.

For new employees this is helped if you have a 'buddy' programme where each new person is linked to someone more experienced who can show them the ropes.

Oh, and some guidelines on relationships at work. It's only fair that everyone knows what is expected of them in any given situation: you can't go rollicking someone for having sex in the broom cupboard if it hasn't been spelt out to them that they don't do that sort of thing – 'But we always did it at my previous place of work and no one complained'.

LET THEM KNOW RIGHT FROM THE OFF WHAT IS EXPECTED OF THEM

Understand the roles of others

I used to believe that to be a good leader I had to be able to do not only my own job – managing – but also everyone else's job as well. And probably, I thought in my heart of hearts, I should be able to do it as well as them if not better. Thus, I figured, if there was an emergency I could step into the breach and do their job and everything would carry on functioning. Yep, I bet you're there before me. If I were to step into their job, who would be doing mine?

Answer, of course: nobody.

The key is to have a practical understanding of what all the jobs entail but realise that you don't need to be able actually to do them. Yes, you do need back-up in the event of a crisis, but it ain't you. You're better off right where you are – leading.

To understand the role, the best way is to know what problems it solves and how it works. But you don't need to be able to do it as well as your team member does – that's what you pay them for. Something about keeping dogs and barking yourself – you need to know what job the guard dog does, but you don't need to go round biting burglars to appreciate it fully.

And often you'll employ someone for such a specialised job you wouldn't know where to begin. You might be the manager of a power plant but you don't need to know how to calculate the shelf life of plutonium. But you do need to know that you employ someone who can do that job for you.

It's also important for all your team to have an understanding of what everyone else does. This certainly helps create a team spirit and a sense of loyalty.

YOU DON'T NEED TO BE ABLE TO DO A ROLE AS WELL AS YOUR TEAM MEMBER DOES – THAT'S WHAT YOU PAY THEM FOR

Understand the pros and cons of individualism

You may have encountered the term 'individualism' before, or you may not. It doesn't matter. The concept is timeless – it's just the jargon that's changed as the approach has become more popular. Essentially it's about prioritising the people in your team as individuals above the needs of the group. You put their financial requirements, need for autonomy and self-expression, their personal goals and so on at the centre of how you manage them.

The opposite approach is known as collectivism, where you consider the needs of the group and the organisation above those of the individual people within it. Autonomy is frowned upon here, and the emphasis is on shared decision-making, collaboration, and the team's goals taking priority over those of its members.

Now, you should be able to see that there are arguments for and against each of these leadership styles. And you should also see that this a spectrum and you don't have to be right down at the individualist end, or out of sight at the collectivist end. What you need to do, as a leader, is to recognise that you can't pick all the good bits out of both options because they're not mutually compatible. You have to make a choice about where your team sits on the spectrum.

Once you know where that sweet spot is, it will inform all sorts of decisions, from the kind of people you're looking for when you hire, to how you recognise achievement, whether you reward your high-achievers differently from others, how the work environment is designed, your attitude to people working remotely and so much more.

So where will you position your team? It will depend on what you're trying to achieve. For example, a more individualistic approach can work well if you're leading a group of creatives, where some people might work best alone, and competitiveness and individual reward and recognition can be productive. On the other hand, this can lead to friction, or anxiety and demotivation in some people.

Collectivism, by contrast, is great when you really need strong teamwork. It rewards group loyalty, and recognises achievements in terms of how they benefit the team as a whole. This can create a positive morale when things go well, and everyone can sense they're part of a successful whole. On the downside, non-conformists and some neurodivergent people can struggle with this approach, and the lack of individual recognition can be demotivating.

So there isn't an objective right or wrong approach, but there will be a better style of leadership for your particular group of people, and you need to understand what it is, and adopt it knowingly for everyone's benefit.

YOU HAVE TO MAKE A CHOICE ABOUT WHERE YOUR TEAM SITS ON THE SPECTRUM

RULE 8

Get the best resources for your team

If your team is a tool you use to get greater glory for little ol' you, then the resources your team uses are the tools it needs to carry it – and thus you – onward and forward. Too many managers think that by cutting their team's resources they are earning some sort of brownie points to be stored up – and used in what? Heaven? I don't think so. You have to get the best resources for your team. By depriving the team you are depriving it also of the chance to shine, to propel you to greater glory.

I know of a lot of managers who say, 'Oh, they can manage for a few more years with this operating system'. Or 'They'd probably just play games all day with a new iPhone, I can save a bob or two if I hold off for a bit'. I have even heard, 'I try to keep a short rein on what they need in case it gets out of hand'.

For heaven's sake. Get your team the best, the very, very best, and then let it get on with its job – which is to make you look good.

If your people need technology – get it for them even if you have to move heaven and earth. If they need more staff, bigger and better machines, higher quality tools – go get 'em. Whatever it is they need to get their job done slicker, quicker, better, bigger, faster, more productively, cheaper, whatever – go get it. If you have to argue, sweat blood, plead, beg, bust a budget or two – do it. Do it now.

You simply can't expect your team to (a) give their best, or (b) be motivated, if you keep them short. They will talk to other people you know: colleagues in the same organisation, friends in other organisations. They will know when they are being short-changed and they will resent it, resent you and work less effectively. In consequence, you will fail to shine. *Ipso facto* – go get them the best you can.

GET YOUR TEAM THE BEST, THE VERY, VERY BEST, AND THEN LET IT GET ON WITH ITS JOB

Be ready to prune

OK, so say you've got an orchestra and you get them to play. You listen. Something wrong somewhere. Yep, that flute player is out of tune, off key and playing from a different hymn sheet. Now you have three choices:

- put up with it
- change it
- end it

Let's have a little look at these three because, as in all things – from relationships, to life, to work, to being a parent – these three choices are the same every single time.

So, you're going to put up with it. This makes your entire orchestra sound flat, out of tune and ill-fitted to do its job properly – that of supplying sweet music to the masses. Your listening public (your objective) will not listen and will accuse you, the orchestra leader, of being a nincompoop* – and they would be right.

OK, so you're going to try to change it. Flute player X gets some retraining. They get sent on a remedial flute course – residential of course. They come back with the right hymn sheet but have decided to switch to the bassoon as they were feeling creatively hemmed in by the flute. Problem sorted. Well done for tackling it.

However, what if their report says they are tone deaf and should never have been in the orchestra in the first place and should have taken up a career sounding the fire alarm somewhere? What you can't do is then embark on another course of action where you give them the triangle to play but they mess that up too and by now the

* They don't of course use this word, but I'm not allowed to use the word they really would use

rest of the orchestra has lost confidence in you and is beginning to mutiny.

Time for the third course. Remove them from the team. It is swift and kind. They can then go on to become a champion alarm ringer somewhere, somewhere else that is, and your orchestra recognises you as decisive, knowing what you want, objective (you put the needs of the many before the bad playing of one) and utterly in charge. Have an extra brownie point.

Always be ready to prune dead wood, straggly growth, lousy flute players (and any other team players who don't cut the mustard).

> **NOW YOU HAVE THREE CHOICES: PUT UP WITH IT, CHANGE IT, END IT**

Make your team better than you

A really good leader – yep, that's you again – knows that when their team takes wing and soars, they too will soar. Getting your team to soar takes courage, grit, determination and an overwhelming passion.

You have to make members of your team better than you, which means trusting them, getting them the best resources, training them to take over from you, trusting them not to stab you in the back when it's time to take over from you and being confident enough in your own abilities not to be jealous of them when they do take off. Tall order.

It takes quite some leader to carry this one out. You have to be pretty relaxed and secure in your own position. Encouraging your team to bring it on takes guts, quite frankly.

Let's take a look at your team. Who've you got there? Which ones will one day fill your shoes? What can you share with them to bring them on?

Shoe-fillers are the ones you want to cultivate and grow. They are the bright ones, the keen ones, the eager beavers. I once had a young assistant who was so sharp he scared me. But when I did move on up, he filled my shoes. And he came with me over several moves, always one step behind. Now the crazy thing was he was better than me in lots of ways but he never chanced his arm and overtook me. It could have been out of respect but I doubt it – the industry I worked in was a little cut-throat to say the least. No, it was habit.

Once you've built a good team it gets in the habit of having you as its leader and then it feels comfortable with that and doesn't mutiny or overtake you. Teams only do that when they feel resentful or mistrusted. So bring 'em on and train 'em up and make 'em better.

> **ONCE YOU'VE BUILT A GOOD TEAM IT GETS IN THE HABIT OF HAVING YOU AS THE MANAGER**

TAKE THE LEAD

Now you have your team around you, you need to make sure they know who's in charge. That's not so you can throw your weight around for the sake of it, it's so you can make sure the system, the team, runs as effectively as possible. You can't have people choosing to do everything in their own way just because they like it, or it's easier, or it's what they're used to, or it's how their old boss did it. This is your team now, and it operates your way. Yes of course – as we'll see later – most people prefer to be set parameters for a task and then be left to do it their way. But who is setting those parameters? You are. You might or might not have discussed it with them first, but you're in control.

Your team needs to know how things work. What they can and can't do, how meetings are run, what to do if they hit problems, how far they can use their own initiative. And just like children, the clearer and more secure they are in this knowledge, the more they can relax. And they'll only be clear if they absolutely accept you as their leader.

So by making it clear who is in charge, and how things operate under your command, you're doing them a favour. You're letting them know where the lines are drawn, so it's easy for them to stay within them.

Set your boundaries

You have to, right from day one, be totally on top of the discipline issue. Remember earlier we talked about how looking after your team can be a bit like being a parent? Well, as a parent you pretty well have to set boundaries and practise zero tolerance to survive. Give 'em an inch and they'll take the whole rope. If you are seen to be 'soft' they'll take advantage. The good thing with clear boundaries and zero tolerance is you have a finite line – a yardstick by which you can judge everything. All you have to do is ask, 'Is this a breach of the rules?' If it is, stop it. If you do allow it, where do you stop?

Say one of your clear boundaries is timekeeping (it might be dress or customer care or personal phone calls, but just say it's timekeeping). If one minute late is fine, what about two? If two is fine, what about three? And so on until people are wandering in at whatever time they feel like. But if you don't allow it, then that's the end of the story. You don't have to think about that particular issue any more. Whereas if you do allow infringements, small breaches, you are forever having to consider, 'Is this a step too far?' 'Can I wrest control back?' 'How far am I prepared to go?'

This doesn't mean you need to have hundreds of rules and be ridiculously inflexible. It means that you need to decide on your few key boundaries that are important to you and to the team and the business. Make them clear. And make them firm.

Remember you are dealing with a team – I will stress this again and again throughout this book – and not an individual. You might feel that for each and any person an exception can be made, but you aren't dealing with individuals – you are dealing with a team. If you are seen to be soft on one individual, then you must be soft on all. If you allow one to wander in late, then all must be allowed to wander in late. If one person can get away with breaking the rules, then all must be allowed.

The good leader is firm on inappropriate behaviour because this sends out a clear message to all the team – the message that you are a good, firm, in-control sort of leader who sets more store by what the team can achieve collectively than by being thought of as an easy-going, laid-back, nice person. Yes, individually some of the team may rate you as pretty cool if you let them get away with murder, but the team will collectively rubbish you.

> THE GOOD THING WITH ZERO TOLERANCE IS YOU HAVE A FINITE LINE – A YARDSTICK BY WHICH YOU CAN JUDGE EVERYTHING

Offload as much as you can – or dare

The good leader, and that is you from now on, knows that they manage events, processes, situations, strategies but never people. Look, let's imagine you have a big garden and decide to employ a gardener. Do you manage the gardener? No. They manage themselves quite nicely, thank you. Your job is to manage the garden. You'll decide what to plant and when and where. The gardener, like a spade or a wheelbarrow, becomes a tool in that garden and a tool you can use to manage your garden effectively. But you don't manage the gardener. They manage themselves. You tell them what you want done and they get on with it. You delegate and they dig and delve and plant and prune and tend and weed. The plants actually manage themselves as well; neither you nor the gardener actually grows anything – you both manage. The gardener is your useful assistant, your tool for getting stuff done.

Now it makes sense to give the gardener as much to do with the decision-making process as possible to free you up for long-term strategy, seeing the big picture, seasonal planning and perusing seed catalogues while sitting in the shade sipping a cooling Pimm's.

There is no point standing over the gardener while they mow lawns, weed beds, prune trees and the like. It is better to give them the job to do and then let them get on with it. Once they have finished you can check their work and make sure it is up to scratch. And then you probably won't need to do that again – don't keep checking.

And that basically is the secret of good leadership. Give 'em a job to do and leave 'em alone. Check once or twice to make sure they've done it the way you want it done and then next time just let them get on with it. Increasingly give them more and more to do and stand back more and more from the people processes and concentrate instead on the planning processes. Build your team and then trust them to get on with it. Sometimes this will backfire and people will play up, skive off, do things badly – and hey, that'll be entirely your fault because you are the manager and it's your team. No, that's serious, it is entirely down to you. Read on and we'll find ways to make sure it doesn't happen – well, not too often anyway.

BUILD YOUR TEAM AND THEN TRUST THEM TO GET ON WITH IT

Know your own importance

You are the most important person in your team, and you'd better know it. No, not because you're a better person or more experienced or more valuable or anything to get big-headed about. You're the most important person because everyone else will take their lead from you. You set the bar.

If you play dirty, backstab, worry that your team members are better than you, spy on them, try to stop them outshining you, or are unethical, disrespectful, or anything else of the sort, then you're not going to excel as a leader. Your team will be so busy checking over their shoulders that they won't perform, and your department won't shine.

Maybe you don't get involved in all that nasty stuff? Good, pleased to hear it. But it won't help much either if you whinge, complain about directors or customers, take a negative view, resist change, talk about how much you're looking forward to Friday afternoon, always take the easy option, avoid hard work – your team will copy all those things instead.

Listen, if you don't set the standard, raise the tone, be the person you want your team to be, then you won't be a truly great leader. Your team is like a flock of birds or sheep or, well, anything that comes in a flock.* Where one goes, they all go. And you're the one they all follow. If you shine, everyone shines. If you fail, everyone fails. Because of you. Scary, huh?

But it's OK. Because you can be that brilliant manager they need to lead them. And when you are, they'll be a brilliant team full of brilliant people. Not only will you succeed personally, but you'll

* Except maybe wallpaper

bring success to everyone around you. You'll approach every task with enthusiasm backed up by solid analysis and common-sense strategies. You'll treat people around you fairly, encourage others, deliver better than you promised and create a positive atmosphere – and so will everyone around you. Because of you.

> **IF YOU DON'T SET THE STANDARD, RAISE THE TONE, BE THE PERSON YOU WANT YOUR TEAM TO BE, THEN YOU WON'T BE A TRULY GREAT LEADER**

Hold effective meetings ...

We've all been to them – the meetings that drag on, people who ramble, agendas written on the back of an envelope or spur of the moment, any-other-business surprises, lack of information, insufficient notice, endless repetition of 'You're on mute …'.

As a manager you have to hold meetings. Make them effective. Decide in advance what the objective of the meeting is and make sure you meet that objective.

Basically, meetings have only four purposes:

- to create and fuse a team
- to impart information
- to brainstorm ideas (and make decisions)
- to collect information (and make decisions)

Some meetings might well take in one or more of these, but you should still be aware of that and add it into your objective. If your meeting is to impart information, then do it and get the hell out. If it's a discussion about that information you want, then that's a different type of meeting and as such should have different objectives.

Be aware that some meetings are there to help your team meet each other, bond, socialise together, find out about each other and see you in your true role as team leader.

If you want your meetings to be effective, then remain firmly in control – no wishy-washy democracies here. You are the chair and you are in charge – end of story. To be effective you shouldn't allow anyone to reminisce, ramble, rabbit on, refuse to shut up or relax. Keep 'em moving fast and get them out of the door as soon as you can.

DECIDE IN ADVANCE WHAT THE OBJECTIVE OF THE MEETING IS AND MAKE SURE YOU MEET THAT OBJECTIVE

... No, really effective

Right, now you're sure this meeting is necessary, and what it's for, let's keep it as brief and effective as possible.

Hold all meetings at the end of the day rather than at the beginning. Everyone's anxious to be off home and it keeps meetings shorter; at the beginning of the day everyone has ages to digress and chat. Unless of course it is a bonding meeting; you can cheerfully hold them at the beginning of business.

See how many meetings you could hold by Zoom, phone, one-to-one (cut out everyone who isn't absolutely essential).

Start all meetings on time. Never wait for anyone. Never go back over stuff for latecomers. If they've missed something vital they can get it from others after the meeting and it'll learn 'em to be on time next time.* Useful tip – never schedule meetings to begin exactly on the hour, always say 3.10 rather than 3 o'clock. You'll find people will always be more punctual if you set an 'odd' time. Try 3.35 if you want to be really wacky.

Schedule the meeting far enough in advance – but not too far – so that no one can say they had something else on. Confirm the day before with everyone to make sure they have remembered and can make it.

---

* The Toad, having finished his breakfast, picked up a stout stick and swung it vigorously, belabouring imaginary animals. 'I'll learn 'em to steal my house!' he cried. 'I'll learn 'em, I'll learn 'em!' 'Don't say "learn 'em," Toad,' said the Rat, greatly shocked. 'It's not good English.' 'What are you always nagging at Toad for?' inquired the Badger, rather peevishly. 'What's the matter with his English? It's the same what I use myself, and if it's good enough for me, it ought to be good enough for you!' 'I'm very sorry,' said the Rat humbly. 'Only I THINK it ought to be "teach 'em", not "learn 'em."' 'But we don't WANT to teach 'em,' replied the Badger. 'We want to LEARN 'em – learn 'em, learn 'em! And what's more, we're going to DO it, too!' (*The Wind in the Willows* by Kenneth Grahame)

You decide who keeps the minutes – and make sure they do, and to your liking. You don't have to be bossy or aggressive about this, just firm, friendly and utterly in control.

Make sure every point on the agenda ends up with an action plan – no action plan means it was just a chat. Or make a decision of course.

You don't do 'any other business' – ever. If it's important it should be on the agenda. If it isn't, then it shouldn't be there at all. 'Any other business' is invariably someone trying to get something over on someone else. Don't allow it – ever.

If regular meetings are getting too big – more than six people – start to subdivide them into committees and get your committees to report back.

And most important of all – engrave this one on your heart – all meetings must have a definite purpose. At the end of the meeting you must be able to say whether or not you met that purpose. Oh yes, and hold all meetings on uncomfortable chairs (or standing) – that speeds things up considerably.

START ALL MEETINGS ON TIME. NEVER WAIT FOR ANYONE

Make meetings fun

I guess that when you were working your way up to your illustrious position of today you had to sit through many interminable meetings, all boring, all stupefyingly dull. Well, the pattern has to be broken somewhere and I'm relying on you to break it. The old way of doing meetings has to stop and you're the very person to do the stopping.

So let's make 'em fun. Now, before we go on, I remember a tip I read somewhere. Basically you were supposed to give out five coins to each meeting member and when they wanted to speak they had to spend a penny. Once they had used up their coins they were done and dusted and couldn't say anything more. It was supposed to make people really cautious about speaking and reluctant to spend all their coins on trivia. Fun? Maybe. But it would also get you quite a reputation as a prat and/or an ineffectual meeting leader. As would other suggestions such as:

- fancy dress
- food and/or drink (unless it's lunchtime, in which case that's functional not fun; or if you take your team out to a restaurant or down the pub, and then it's not a meeting, it's a bonding session – or a thank you of course)
- games, quizzes or contests of any sort
- having small surprises such as chocolates strapped under the chairs
- a talking stick (don't ask)
- blindfolds
- letting the most junior member chair the meeting

All of these head towards farce, ruin and idiocy. Don't go there.

So how can you fun things up without making yourself look ridiculous? Well, for a start, fun doesn't have to mean silly or stupid or unfunny.

Fun means not being stuffy, allowing people to be themselves and to bring their own contribution. Fun means allowing people to share things that have made them laugh without being frowned on. Fun is about letting people tell stories or anecdotes that lighten the mood (just know when to say, 'Right, back to business'). Fun means being flexible enough to allow other suggestions as to where and how you all meet. Perhaps your organisation has a great boardroom – could you meet there? Or outside if the weather is good.

The confident leader – that's you – can be flexible because they are relaxed and cool and confident. The stuffy manager is frightened because they feel insecure and seek a rigid approach to prop up their lack of self-confidence.

> THE OLD WAY OF DOING MEETINGS HAS TO STOP AND YOU'RE THE VERY PERSON TO DO THE STOPPING

Listen to ideas from others

If you think you know it all, chances are you will be too busy listening to yourself and how great you are to have time to listen to anyone else. But I know that's not you. Everyone, no matter how lowly their position or task, has something to offer you. Try talking to the lift operator, the car park attendant, the canteen staff, the cleaning staff, whoever and whatever. And, most important, listen to people in your team. They are the ones in the know who have to work with the resources and the products. They are the ones at the cutting edge and they may well have ideas, good ideas. You don't need to consult them over every little thing but the big things ... well, yes. Talk to them. Get their feedback, their ideas, their creativity.

You obviously have to be careful to make sure that although you are listening to them it is you who still carries the can. You might listen but that doesn't mean you are going to act on every one of their ideas. Nip in the bud the feeling that if they suggest, you have to carry out. Therein lies terrible trouble. Listen, assimilate and then decide based on what you've heard, your own experience and ideas and what is practical. It's no good you listening and then not using their information and them becoming terribly despondent –'What's the use of telling the boss my ideas, they're never used?'.

You have to listen without giving the idea that you will necessarily use their ideas, so then they won't be disappointed when you do something completely different. But you can make them think their ideas were incorporated into your overall strategy.

Virtually every team member I have ever known could tell their manager something useful about what they as a team or a company are getting wrong, or how something could be done better.

If you're open to this, ask good questions, and listen without prejudice (or talking over them), you're immediately in a different class to most leaders.

TALK TO THEM. GET THEIR FEEDBACK, THEIR IDEAS, THEIR CREATIVITY

RULE 18

Don't always have to have the last word

Yes, yes, I know you are the boss, the leader – and a damn good one, may I say – but you don't always have to have the last word. This isn't like being kids in the playground.

If people in your team disagree with you openly, then there are two possible reasons why: either they feel confident enough to engage in debate (in which case you ought to appreciate that) or they are out of line and you aren't imposing discipline enough to stop them. It may well be a warning sign that things are wrong or a sign that things are very right – only you can judge.

If they are out of line and there's a discipline issue, obviously you need to deal with that in private. Otherwise, remember that your staff are grown-ups. You have to give them room to be real people and that means they will sometimes disagree, argue and get cross. That's fine in a good team where people can sound off and nobody takes umbrage. It obviously doesn't work in a poor team.

It doesn't pay always to have the last word or always to be right or always to correct staff on every little thing. Sometimes, whether they are right or wrong, it's best to let it go. Know the difference between things important enough that you need to have the last word, and things where it really doesn't matter.

REMEMBER THAT YOUR STAFF ARE GROWN-UPS. YOU HAVE TO GIVE THEM ROOM TO BE REAL PEOPLE

Have clear expectations

One leader I worked with was very moody. When she was relaxed, everyone was productive but had fun. Occasional high jinks kept their spirits up and she didn't have a problem with it, in moderation. When she was stressed, however, you could get your head bitten off for as little as laughing too loud.

As I say, there were times she was very relaxed. But no one else on her team was. They had no idea what mood she'd be in so they were always on tenterhooks. Would she be happy with a report that was poorly presented but contained all the facts, or would she rather wait until tomorrow and have it looking perfect? Could you get away with the briefest of paperwork for a particular procedure, or did you need to fill it in in triplicate, dotting every i and crossing every t? Hard to say really – it depended which side of the bed she got out of that morning.

And how did her team respond? Well, if you've ever worked for a manager like that, you'll know the answer. They were pretty demoralised, and their standards were hugely inconsistent. Obviously, because their manager's standards were similarly wide-ranging.

Look, if your team don't know what your standards are, how can they aspire to them? They're looking to you to set the lead, and if you don't, they can't tell where they're going or how they're supposed to get there. You have to be consistent in the standards you set and the performance you expect. If something is unacceptable on Monday at 10am, it should be unacceptable on Friday at 4pm. If paperwork is supposed to be filled out a particular way, that's the way it should be done every day of the week.

It may sound unreasonable to have a basic standard and then suddenly, for no consistent reason, to expect more of people. And so it is. But it's just as unfair to let them get away with less just because you're in a particular mood. You're not being nice to them – you're confusing them. And you're failing to ensure your team always produces work of the highest standard. And how fair is it to let one person get away with scrappy presentation when their colleague was expected to produce a polished document last week? No, the only way to ensure good morale among your team, and to make sure it turns in a consistently strong performance, is for you to be consistent in enforcing the standards that you set.

And if you ask me next week, I'll tell you exactly the same.

> IF SOMETHING IS UNACCEPTABLE ON MONDAY AT 10AM, IT SHOULD BE UNACCEPTABLE ON FRIDAY AT 4PM

Don't try justifying stupid systems

I was travelling on the railway the other day (yes, there are still some of us who do) when we encountered a problem. It was fairly simple. Someone had messed with a security door at the buffet and triggered an alarm – or something. This brought the train to a standstill, probably quite rightly. But it did this in a very long tunnel. The train couldn't move until the fault had been rectified, which involved finding the train manager (they used to be called guards, remember?) and getting him to reset the triggered alarm. All fairly simple.

I was running very late for a meeting, so asked if there wasn't a better system – e.g. letting the buffet staff reset the alarm. The train manager spent about 20 minutes justifying why this system was the best for everyone concerned: him, the buffet staff, the train authorities – everyone, that is, except me, the poor passenger. Much better if he'd just said, 'Yes, it's a useless system and I shall recommend we change it. Thank you for your concern'.

And I bet you have a dozen useless systems within your organisation – we all do. Best not try to justify them. If you can't change them, put up with it, get on with it, but don't try hoodwinking the staff into thinking it's all fab. It isn't, and you lose respect and trust if you try convincing people that it's fine when they know it's not.

I'm not saying you should go round lamenting loudly everything that is bad about your company – far from it, that road only leads to ruin. Remember, if you can't say something nice, best not to say anything at all. Just don't try justifying something you know is stupid, especially to your team.

DON'T TRY HOODWINKING THE STAFF INTO THINKING IT'S ALL FAB

Embrace technology

The pace of technological advance can be dizzying, and as a leader it can feel like a challenge to keep on top of it all. How do you keep your skills up to speed when the technology evolves constantly? You have a whole team, department, company to lead here. Where are you supposed to find the time to familiarise yourself with every new platform, digital tool, AI development?

First off, don't panic. As a leader, your attitude to technology is way more important than your proficiency in any particular area. You need to be positive, open-minded and enthusiastic about new technologies in order to reap the benefits, and so that your team will be motivated by your enthusiasm for new ideas – digital or otherwise.

The only relevance of any technology is what it can do for you. That's true of being able to make fire, of the wheel, the spinning jenny – every technological advance throughout history. So that's the bit you need to understand.

I remember a friend back in the 1980s launching a successful business using early computer games models as a teaching tool. This particular friend didn't own a computer, and had no idea how they worked. But he understood what they could *do*. That's all he needed. It's about seeing the benefits, not about being able to manipulate the software.

So what can new technology do for you? The right developments have the power to simplify analytics for you, engage customers, automate processes, run schedules, collect and collate feedback, solve problems, calculate risks, make decisions, design training, and on and on and on. Those are the benefits you're looking for. Once you can see the potential, you can train up or hire someone else to implement the actual task.

So stay up to speed with industry trends and developments – surely you're doing this anyway? Don't jump on everything just because it's new, but focus on what will help you achieve your goals. Have people around you who understand the nitty gritty of the technology, and hold regular reviews with your team every few months where you all discuss new tech that might be relevant.

As a leader with a forward-looking attitude, you can inspire your team members to look for opportunities. Get them searching for innovative solutions to sit alongside the department's strategic goals. Once they know you welcome new technology – where it's useful – you can train them to assess which approaches are genuinely helpful, to analyse the pros and cons, and to learn any new skills the department needs. You see? No need to do it all yourself.

> **THE ONLY RELEVANCE OF ANY TECHNOLOGY IS WHAT IT CAN DO FOR YOU**

Be ready to say yes

The good leader – that's you – tries to stay completely fresh. Not to get stuck in the same old ways of doing things. That means not having a default mechanism of 'No, we don't do it like that'. Instead replace it with 'That's an interesting idea. How do you think that would work?'.

What's more, you need to encourage people to come up with new ideas, as well as coming up with them yourself. Try ideas out. Take one new idea each week and give it a go. It might be fairly simple, 'We'd like more choice of biscuits with our morning tea, please', or something radical, 'Listen up, guys, we're going to try a completely new approach to sales and distribution'.

Obviously it makes sense to try out smaller ideas first to make sure your team can cope well with change, and then move on to the more radical ones later. Break 'em in slowly.

And as fast as you are introducing new ideas, get your team to do the same with their own individual jobs so that they don't grow stale either. If everyone has a new idea each week, that's a whole big bunch of new ideas by the end of the year for themselves and for the whole team. 'I just thought I could speed the process up if I … ' 'Wow, I could take that idea and adapt it to my work station and then I could … ' 'Yeah, and I bet they'd be really interested in this in accounts because it could simplify the whole … ' And so on.

Biggest challenge? Getting your team on side – everyone is resistant to change initially. If you flag, the whole team will also flag.

If you maintain the passion, the whole team will be infected and become addicted to this. Believe me. Trust me. I know you already have enough to do, but we'll move on to delegating in a bit and that'll free up some time. Then you'll have more time to do this, which, in a way, is part of your real job – managing.

Encourage innovation. Reward good ideas. Create a culture where ideas are recognised (even if not adopted) and valued.

IF EVERYONE HAS A NEW IDEA EACH WEEK, THAT'S A WHOLE BIG BUNCH OF NEW IDEAS BY THE END OF THE YEAR

Give credit to the team when it deserves it

Just as you must always stand up and take the blame, so too must you always heap praise and credit on your team when things go well. If that fabulous sale to Client X comes off because you happened to stay up all night working on it and then used an old contact from a previous job and then swung it because you happened to know something the competition didn't – why, then you say, 'The team did it'.

Taking the blame does generate loads of loyalty, but so too does giving the team the credit. Say it loudly, in public, sincerely, but do say it. And don't do it tongue in cheek with 'My team did it', as if you are giving it credit but making sure everyone knows who really was responsible. Everyone knows it is your team so there is no need to mention it, ever. It is OK to say, 'It did a great job, it is a fantastic team. I'm incredibly lucky to have it'. This implies you had nothing to do with it and yet everyone knows it is your team and you are its leader so the team will love you and everyone else will think you incredibly humble and self-effacing. Well done you.

Again, all this takes courage and a lot of self-confidence, I know. You work hard and it doesn't seem fair to give the credit away. I know that you really want to stand up and shout, 'Look, it was me, I did this, all by myself, OK?' But you can't.

You see, you didn't do it all by yourself, no matter how much you might believe that. If you are selling, then it is the team that built the product you are selling. Without that team you would have rubbish to sell. Tell the team that selling the product was a doddle because it had done such a good job. It will glow with pride and redouble its efforts.

WITHOUT THAT TEAM YOU WOULD HAVE RUBBISH TO SELL

Train them to bring you solutions, not problems

It's terribly easy for staff to moan. I think it becomes a habit. You have to train your staff not just to moan. You can allow moaning but insist that if they bring you a problem they must also suggest a solution to the problem. Any idea that there is something wrong should always be met with, 'And what would you like me to do about it?'. If they complain, meet them with, 'What do you think we should do?'.

The best manager I ever worked for carried this even further and made us tell him the solution first – and then let him guess what he thought our 'problem' was. It made it a game, which was sort of fun, but it also made us think on our feet a bit – made us be a bit lateral in our moaning. I was having a problem with security staff. I thought they were wiping the CCTV footage without watching it, which was not on. This was my problem because if anything had happened I would have carried the can. I needed them to watch carefully and couldn't devise a solution to this problem – but I couldn't just go to the boss and moan that they weren't doing their job properly. I had to come up with a solution first.

Then it dawned on me that I didn't need to go to the boss. I could solve this one myself. I had to make sure the security staff thought there was something worth watching. I mentioned that some members of staff had been reported as having sex somewhere on the premises and it could have been covered by the CCTV cameras, but no one was sure by which camera. There were cameras covering car parks, offices, corridors and storage areas in the basement. Result. The security bods started watching as if their lives depended on it. My boss was pleased because this was part of my job brief and he had noticed it wasn't being done properly and was going to pull me up on it. And I had come up with a solution to a problem without going to my boss and just moaning, 'Oh, the security people aren't doing their job properly … '.

Admittedly I had to come up with a fresh solution once the security staff realised they weren't going to see any smutty pictures – but it took them a long time, and they kept going back just in case …

> ANY IDEA THAT THERE IS SOMETHING WRONG SHOULD ALWAYS BE MET WITH, 'AND WHAT WOULD YOU LIKE ME TO DO ABOUT IT?'

DEAL WITH PEOPLE

We all have to work with people. These may be loosely known as a team or a department or a squad or a crew – even a posse. It doesn't matter. The mistake a lot of leaders make is to think they are managing people. They think that people are their tools, their stock-in-trade. Make the people successful and you have the successful leader – or so the theory goes.

But unfortunately this is a myth and we need to see that the real role of the leader is to manage processes rather than people. People can manage themselves if you let them. What you need to be concentrating on is the real job of management – the strategy. The team is merely a means to fulfilling that end. If all your people could be replaced by machines – and how many of us haven't prayed that this might happen? – we would still have to have a strategy, still have to be leading the process.

Of course we, as leaders, have to work with real flesh-and-blood people and we have to know what motivates them, how they think and feel, why they come to work, why they give their best (or their worst), what they are afraid of, what they hope for and dream of. We will have to encourage them, coach them, give them the resources to do their job and manage themselves, oversee their processes and set their strategy for them. We will worry about them, look out for them, be on their side and support them. But we won't manage them. We will let them manage themselves and we shall concentrate on our real role as a leader.

Get them emotionally involved

You lead people. People who are paid to do a job. But if it is 'just a job' to them, you'll never get their best. If they come to work looking to clock in and clock off and do as little as they can get away with in-between, then you're doomed to failure, my friend. On the other hand, if they come to work looking to enjoy themselves, looking to be stretched, challenged, inspired and to get involved, then you are in with a big chance of getting the very best out of them. Trouble is, the jump from drudge to super team is entirely down to you. It is *you* that has to inspire them, lead them, motivate them, challenge them, get them emotionally involved.

That's OK. You like a challenge yourself, don't you? The good news is that getting a team emotionally involved is easy. All you have to do is make them care about what they are doing. And that's easy too. You have to get them to see the relevance of what they are doing, how it makes an impact on people's lives, how they provide for the needs of other human beings, how they can reach out and touch people by what they do at work. Get them convinced – because it is true of course – that what they do makes a difference, that it contributes to society in some way rather than just lines the owner's or shareholders' pockets, or ensures that the chief executive gets a big fat pay cheque.

And yes, I know it's easier to show how they contribute if you manage nurses rather than an advertising sales team, but if you think about it, then you can find value in any role and instil pride in those who do whatever job it is. Prove it? OK. Well, those who sell advertising space are helping other companies, some of which may be very small, reach their markets. They are alerting potential customers to things they may have wanted for a long time and may really need. They are keeping the newspaper or magazine afloat – and its staff employed – as it relies on ad sales income, and that magazine or newspaper delivers information and/or gives pleasure to the people who buy it (otherwise they wouldn't, would they?).

Get them to care because that's an easy thing to do. Look, this is a given. Everyone deep down wants to be valued and to be useful. The cynics will say this is nonsense, but it is true, deep down true. All you have to do is reach down far enough and you will find care, feeling, concern, responsibility and involvement. Drag all that stuff up and they'll follow you forever and not even realise why.

Oh, just make sure that you've convinced yourself first before you try this out on your team. Do you believe that what you do makes a positive difference? If you're not sure, reach down, deep down, and find a way of caring ...

GET THEM CONVINCED – BECAUSE IT IS TRUE OF COURSE – THAT WHAT THEY DO MAKES A DIFFERENCE

Encourage them

If you don't let people know you're pleased with them, they'll wilt. People come to work for a whole raft of reasons – most, nothing to do with the money despite what they'll tell you – and right there at the top of their unwritten, unspoken, undeclared list will be 'Praise from the boss'. That's you by the way, the boss.

They might call it 'recognition' or 'acknowledgement' or 'feeling I've done well' – but how do they know? They know because you tell them.

Now you can praise them retroactively, so to speak – wait until they've done good and then tell them they've done good – or you can encourage them in advance – active praise. Tell them they're going to do good before they've done it. Why? Because the chances of them doing good are that much greater if you have praised them in advance. They won't want to let you down, or themselves.

Being a leader is a minimalist's dream. You want to build a great team and you want to do it with the smallest output of resources. Praise is free. It is instantly replaceable, doesn't wear out, is invariably 100 per cent effective, is incredibly simple to do and takes no time at all.

So why don't more leaders do it? Because it takes self-assurance. You have to be feeling pretty good about yourself to be able to dish out praise well in advance. If you doubt yourself, you'll doubt them. If you doubt them, you'll not praise them because you'll be sure they are going to screw up.

It takes nothing except courage to say, 'Come on, you can do it. You'll be fine'. The more responsibility you give people, the more you trust them, the more you praise them, the more you encourage them, the more they'll give you in return. Praise costs nothing and brings in loads. Encouragement should be a given.

Just keep it genuine. If you tell them they've done brilliantly when they know they haven't, you devalue the currency. It helps to be specific and pick out the bits that were brilliant: 'You handled the customer beautifully; they were practically thanking you for losing the original order'. They'll value that more than a generic 'Well done, good stuff' too.

Encourage an atmosphere where everyone encourages everyone else – 'You can do it' should be heard every day all around you. If you're not saying it, chances are your team isn't either. Encourage the good ones to give the less good ones a hand up. In any good team an air of fostering help should be actively encouraged and praised when it happens. We're all in this together and we sink or swim together.

TELL THEM THEY'RE GOING TO DO GOOD BEFORE THEY'VE DONE IT

Set realistic targets – no, really realistic

When I was doing the research for this book, someone said that setting realistic targets was unrealistic and that all targets should be 'stretching' ones because that would impress the board. Now, can you see the problem here? Yep, we're not talking here about motivating a team, getting a job done, creating an atmosphere of success and creativity. No, we're talking about impressing the board. Now on paper that might be a smart thing to do if your board is made up of monkeys, but I bet it isn't. I bet it's made up of pretty shrewd cookies who would see through a manoeuvre like that in a nanosecond.

When I say realistic, I don't say lower or easy-to-achieve targets. I say realistic. That might mean taxing. It might mean a struggle. It might mean your team has to redouble its efforts, work harder, longer, brighter. But it has to be realistic and that means achievable, within your grasp. And yes, you might have to stretch a bit.

Realistic means you know what your team is capable of and what is expected of it by your bosses. Somehow you will have to marry the two to keep both sides happy. You can't pressurise your team out of existence, nor can you let your bosses think you're slacking.

If your bosses insist on setting targets that aren't realistic, you must feed that back to them. Don't argue or procrastinate – feed it back to them. Ask how they think the targets could be achieved. Say they are unrealistic. Be very well prepared, make your case that the targets are unrealistic and ask again how they think they could be achieved. Suggest a realistic target of your own, well supported by facts and figures. Keep feeding the problem back to your bosses and asking for clarification. Sooner or later they must set a more realistic target or order you to achieve the impossible. Either way, you are absolved of the problem. If they set you realistic targets, then all you need to do is meet those targets (you know you can do this). If they order you to fulfil unrealistic ones, you are also in the clear – when you fail to achieve the unachievable you will be able to explain that at the time you did register your protest and bring your case back to them.

KEEP FEEDING THE PROBLEM BACK TO YOUR BOSSES

Accept their limitations

As we saw earlier, effectively fusing a team together means you need several different parts – or team members. Now some of us are good at certain things and others not so. If we were all the same we wouldn't be able to work as a team – we would all be leaders or all followers and you need a combination, not either/or.

So if some members of your team aren't leaders – or followers – you have to accept that. If some are good at figure work and others not, you have to accept that. If some are good at working unsupervised and others not, you have to accept that.

And to be able to accept these things you have to know your staff pretty well. You have to know their strengths and weaknesses, good points and bad. If you don't – and I'm sure this doesn't apply to you – you will be forever trying to shove round pegs into square holes and vice versa.

You have to accept that not everyone is going to be as bright, as determined, as ambitious, as clever or as motivated as you are – praise indeed from me. Some of your team are quite possibly going to be brain dead from the feet up and you might need to practise Rule 9 before this one if there simply is no hope. But don't act in haste. You might not need a team of geniuses (in fact if you hire people far too smart for a job, they will just leave, fast).

Suppose your team contains machine operators or admin assistants. Now you don't need these good people to have Einstein brains nor to be really on the ball when it comes to brainstorming. But you do need them to be able to sit in an arse-numbing position for hours at a time concentrating on a bit of work that would drive you or me batty. Just don't go expecting them to take creative wing and soar away with new ideas, new innovations or new technologies. You have to accept their limitations, and love them for them because these limitations are their parameters by which you can get the very best out of them – their best of course. And while you're at it, have a quick check of your own limitations. What's that? You haven't got any? Come on.

IF WE WERE ALL THE SAME WE WOULDN'T BE ABLE TO WORK AS A TEAM – WE WOULD ALL BE LEADERS OR ALL FOLLOWERS

Celebrate

I find an excuse every day to reward my people with a little something – a modest celebration for a result no matter how small, how trivial it seems. If you do the same, you'll have a motivated staff who have a habit of celebrating every success. And that's so important.

And the rewards? Tiny. A box of doughnuts. Extra froth on their cappuccinos. A chance to go outside and sit in the sun.

Sometimes I declare today a special day because we just got such and such a result and then I take them out to lunch, let them take time off, let them tell me their worst jokes – never all at the same time, mind.

And, occasionally, I declare such a special day even if we fail to win an order. I reward mistakes, screw-ups, failures, accidents. Why? Well, they've all slogged their guts out, done their best, given their all, sold their grannies and sweated blood. Why shouldn't I reward them? Just because we failed doesn't mean we didn't strive. I am rewarding the effort. I am celebrating all that we did right – effort, struggle, determination, teamwork, drive and good honest labour.

Don't just celebrate the big wins, celebrate all the little ones as well – obviously with smaller celebrations, but celebrations of some sort nevertheless. Hey, any excuse to go and get a coffee. And a bag of doughnuts (or apples if they like). What does that cost you? Very little, but the warm feeling it generates far exceeds any cost.

WHY SHOULDN'T I REWARD THEM? JUST BECAUSE WE FAILED DOESN'T MEAN WE DIDN'T STRIVE

Create a good atmosphere

Creating a good atmosphere isn't only easy but also essential. If your team are sullen and despondent and depressed and surly – it shows. It shows in their work, the way they handle customers and colleagues, the way they relate to each other and, most importantly, the way they work with you and for you.

It takes nothing to say good morning politely and mean it. It isn't a chore to make sure everyone has got a coffee or tea for a meeting. It takes a second to ask, 'How are you today?' The three rules for any workplace are:

- politeness
- friendliness
- kindness

Yep, we've all known the bosses who shout and are rude and belligerent but, like the dinosaurs, they are a dying breed and we can move on. People are entitled to:

- respect
- civilised behaviour
- dignity

If you can't give them these things you shouldn't be a leader. But I'm sure you can. Creating a good atmosphere is easy. It comes from the top down. It is your job and your responsibility to be cheerful, considerate, polite and helpful. Your people are one of your most important resources – your tools, your weapons of mass achievement. Without them you are nothing. With them you are a team. Use them kindly and don't abuse them. Be genuinely interested in them and their lives. If you don't have time – make time.

I guess the word I am looking for is 'courtesy'. An old-fashioned concept, I'll grant you, but one that gets mountains moved, doors opened and staff working shifts they would normally have refused to do.

WITHOUT THEM YOU ARE NOTHING. WITH THEM YOU ARE A TEAM

Inspire loyalty and team spirit

If you work together, chances are you are seeing more of your team than you are of your family. And your team is seeing more of you than of their families. If this is the case you had better all get on. Now you don't have to love each other, but you do have to be a family. And the best way to do that is to inspire loyalty and create a team spirit. You, as the leader, have to be the head of the family.

You have to be respected, looked up to, trusted and relied upon. Tall order. Strong stuff. Can you do all that? Course you can. All you have to do is:

- reward them
- praise them
- be kind to them
- trust them
- inspire them
- lead them
- motivate them
- develop them
- genuinely care about them

These are the kinds of things that are easier to say than to do, and there's a temptation for you to skip down the list saying 'Yes, yes, I do that'. Now take a minute and go back and really think about each one. Do you *really* do that? Could you do it better? Are you absolutely sure you don't *think* you do it, but perhaps not actually do it? What people think they do and what they actually do can be very different indeed. Find somebody you can ask for honest feedback. Ideally one of your team – if not, somebody who sees you with your team. What do they say you do?

I once worked in competition with another company. One of their leader's team lived with one of my team. She told John, my team member, all her boss's plans, figures, results, future promotions etc., and I was able to beat him every time. Now why didn't she pass on all my stuff to her boss, seeing as she obviously discussed work with John? Simple. She didn't like her manager. And that was his fault entirely. He was rude to his team, abusive, uncooperative and unkind. Was I a soft touch? No way. I was strict and businesslike but I treated my team with respect. I didn't have to do much because my competitor was doing enough wrong to make me look good.

CHANCES ARE YOU ARE SEEING MORE OF YOUR TEAM THAN YOU ARE OF YOUR FAMILY

Have and show trust in your staff

You have a computer, and it crashes from time to time – that's a given. You have a car. It breaks down from time to time, even if it's only a puncture – that, too, is a given. Now you don't eye either of these warily, expecting them to let you down, watching them like a hawk in case they show any sign of breaking down, do you? No, of course not. So stop watching your team like that. They are a tool for getting a job done. They will break down, crash, whatever, from time to time but we accept their limitations – Rule 28 – and we allow them to make mistakes – Rule 66 – and we accept that we aren't managing them but their processes instead.

And if you can make that move to trusting your team you must show them that you are doing exactly that. Trust not only has to be done but it also has to be seen to be done. Sometimes you'll have to make a big show of really leaving them alone to get on with it.

You show them that you trust them by backing off, leaving them alone to get on with the job. Stop peering over their shoulders, checking every few moments, looking up nervously every time they move or cough or get up. Relax and let them get on with it. You can still ask them to report back at the end of the day/week and encourage them to come to you to discuss any problems. Just make it clear you trust them to do it, and you are always there if they need support or guidance.

But, I hear you say, what if I really don't trust them? What if I know they're a lazy, good-for-nothing, shiftless bunch of liberty takers? What if, indeed? Whose team is it? Who employed, trained, kept such a bunch of monkeys?

Sorry, bit harsh, but sometimes we need to face the reality. If you can't trust your team you need to look to your own leadership skills – or keep reading. A good team leader (that's you) has a good team following them. If the team is faulty, then the leadership has to be challenged. If the team is right, you can trust it. If the team really can't be trusted (and are you *sure* about that?) then it needs to be changed.

YOU SHOW THEM THAT YOU TRUST THEM BY BACKING OFF, LEAVING THEM ALONE TO GET ON WITH THE JOB

Respect individual differences

I have several children. I expect them to operate as a team. But I am also shrewd enough to realise they are all completely different and if I try to treat them all the same, apply the same rules – apart from the discipline ones – I'll get a mutiny, or chaos. Now one of them – and I'm not mentioning any names here but they will know which one I'm talking about – can't be hurried. Not ever, not anyhow. If you shove, he digs his heels in and can't be shifted. He has to be lured, enticed, seduced into being quicker. But I have another child who constantly has to be slowed down. I have to respect – and work with – their individual differences. I simply have to.

Now your team is just the same. Some members can be hurried and others can't. Some will need to be slowed down and others you need to speed up. Some will come to work with a cheery smile, others are best not approached first thing in the morning. Some will be brilliant with technology and others won't. Go back to what Belbin says in Rule 1 and see how everybody in a team has something different to offer – and that difference is what makes your team superb.

With my children if I need something doing fast I know who to call on. If I need a slower, more methodical approach I select another child.

You don't have to let anyone get away with anything just because they are different – keep the discipline rules in place – it's more in the way you treat individual differences, the way you select tasks and the way you expect those tasks to be carried out. We are all different, thank God – a world populated by people like me, even I realise, would be ghastly – and those differences are what make a great team pull together effectively.

So if you're leading a sales team, say, and most of the members are sharp-suited and have slick patter (like you), but one prefers casual garb and is more chatty with her customers, don't mark her cards as 'not a company person' – judge her on the results she gets. If she makes her targets and her customers love her, then *vive la différence*.

DIFFERENCES ARE WHAT MAKE A GREAT TEAM PULL TOGETHER EFFECTIVELY

Adapt your style to each team member

Adapting your style does not mean you have to be a chameleon. It means you have to be sensitive to your team's individuality and work with it. You may have outgoing members who like to be praised in public and then you might have quieter, more introspective members who would shrivel up and die if praised in public and prefer to be told they are doing a good job privately. There, you've changed your style without changing your skin, spots or personality.

I have one team member, a very good one, who does her job superbly but who absolutely hates appraisals and would do anything to get out of them. She loathes having to talk about herself in any way – and this borders almost on a real phobia. I have to change my style with her considerably when carrying out a six-monthly appraisal because if she gets wind of the fact that I'm even thinking about doing one she'll hyperventilate and have a panic attack. And then I have another team member who greets me each morning with a very cheery, 'How am I doing, Boss?' Now he really likes talking about himself and would happily be given a daily appraisal – if I were to let it happen. Both team members do their job extremely well – they wouldn't be there if they didn't – but they do need handling in a completely different way. I want them both to continue doing good work, and I have to handle them differently to get the best from them.

Similarly, some people like to be left alone, to create opportunities and make things happen, and they will come and tell you if they need help (the bright self-motivators) and others will need you to direct their actions more and give them specific projects to do. Don't overmanage the former – they'll resist and they'll get irritated (and quite possibly leave). Equally, don't undermanage the latter or they will feel stressed by a lack of structure to their job and won't work hard. Think about the individual. Think about what they need and what motivates them, and adapt your leadership style accordingly.

> **YOU HAVE TO BE SENSITIVE TO YOUR TEAM'S INDIVIDUALITY AND WORK WITH IT**

Encourage team members to embrace their differences

Everyone is different, and then some people are very different. There's a lot more awareness than there used to be of neurodivergence, and quite rightly too. However it shouldn't matter whether someone is or isn't neurodivergent, or whether they do or don't have a formal diagnosis. The fact is that some people are noticeably outside the norm in certain behaviours, and by that I mean the rest of the team will have noticed it.

Some neurodivergent behaviours can be really quite tricky to work alongside, as indeed can some neurotypical behaviours. We all have our foibles, as the last couple of Rules have indicated. Broadly speaking, whether someone is labelled as ADHD, ASC or anything else should be entirely up to them. In terms of how the team relates to any of its members' more challenging behaviour, the big difference I see is in how much you can expect them to be able to change.

Suppose one of your team gets quite distressed when the coffee station gets messy. Do you tell them to get over it, all coffee stations get messy, and if they don't like it they can clean it up? Or do you sympathise and ask the rest of the team to make sure the coffee station is kept tidy? Of course you're always looking for a compromise that recognises everyone's perspective, but your approach will surely be influenced by whether the team member in question is being needlessly picky, or whether they have diagnosed OCD. Of course, you don't always know the answer to this, but if your antennae are well tuned, you should have a pretty good hunch. Certainly you should always be open to the possibility that some people have genuine, recognised conditions that make things like a messy coffee station – or tight deadlines, or noisy offices, or new people, or changes in routine – much harder to handle.

You can't ask everyone to prove they have a particular condition – they may not even realise it themselves – but you can make sure you're not riding roughshod over their needs. Don't expect them to behave a certain way just because other people are managing to do so. And more than that, you can let your team know that you expect consideration for people's differences. The culture you engender as leader should be one of valuing what everyone contributes, and accepting that we all need to be tolerant of differences, and support each other where necessary, so everyone is free to get on with what they're good at.

It's not an exact science – sometimes two people's genuine needs aren't compatible with each other and you have to be very smart, and very thoughtful, to keep things working smoothly. But that's your job. Anyone can be a leader when everything's going right. Having said that, you make your job much easier if you've established a culture of tolerance and acceptance, because everyone will feel heard, and will want to find a solution.

YOU MAKE YOUR JOB MUCH EASIER IF YOU'VE ESTABLISHED A CULTURE OF TOLERANCE AND ACCEPTANCE

Let them think they know more than you (even if they don't)

This one is so simple and yet I bet very few leaders use it. And why not? It makes people feel really special and important. All you have to do is say to your staff, 'You know about this, what do you think?'. The key principles to this rule are:

- ask their opinion
- get their ideas and views
- give them more responsibility than they ever had before – you'll be surprised how people always rise to a challenge
- discuss important issues and news with them
- encourage feedback
- never dismiss them as being 'mere workers'

Even if you *know* you know more about a subject than they do – still do it. They feel good. They perform better. They learn from your conversations. Maybe you learn too.

And while you're doing all this, take them through the entire process of your industry so that they don't get stuck in a rut of one department. You have to let them see their important role in the overall scheme of things, how their contribution is valuable and helpful and how the whole thing would flounder without them. That's all part of getting them emotionally involved (Rule 25).

Treat them as you would a valuable client you were showing round. Let them in on your industry's secrets: 'Well, we use the new XP8 coatings on our silicon chips, unlike Mathers and Crowley who still use the old XP5, but I expect you know that anyway, but do keep it under your hat as it's how we stole a march on them and got that huge contract with the DVLA last year'.

Keep them informed about developments in your industry – perhaps you could subscribe to your industry's newsletters and magazines, technical journals and papers, that sort of thing – so that they think you are assuming they are interested, informed, know more than perhaps they do. This will encourage them to keep learning and wanting to know more.

> ENCOURAGE THEM TO KEEP LEARNING AND WANTING TO KNOW MORE

Use positive reinforcement

If your staff do something good, tell them. And then tell them again. And again. Keep it up. Put it in writing. Send them a memo – something they can keep. Put it in the company newsletter. Add a note to their file. Whatever, but make it widely known they did good. This is a quick – and cheap (important, with your limited budget) – method of praising and motivating your team (and individual members of course) and it lets everyone know you are monitoring, praising, motivating.

When you praise people, make it simple. If they worked late to get a special order out, say, 'Thank you for working late, we couldn't have done it without you. Your positive response to a difficult situation made everyone's job (especially mine) a lot easier. Thank you'.* That's a whole lot easier than, 'On the evening of the 7th you were seconded to implement an extra shift duty, which you carried out in accordance with our wishes and for which we wish to convey our gratitude, blah, blah … '

Let them know why you are thanking them – 'you made my job easier' – rather than just thanking them for what they did – 'you came in for an extra shift'.

Be personal. Use 'I' and 'we', not 'management'. And say 'thank you' in the same way as you would speak. 'I want to thank you' is so much better than 'The management wishes to express its gratitude'. Who speaks like that?

Praise as soon as the job was done, not a week later – do it the next day at the latest. And do it every time people do something beyond their normal brief. If they are asked to work an extra shift every week, that is just a part of their normal working pattern. Instead, we

---

* Reinforce by saying 'thank you' again

are talking here of the extraordinary, the beyond the normal, going that extra mile sort of stuff.

If you reinforce positive behaviour in this way you will almost certainly guarantee it happening again. Fail to notice, to comment, to praise, and chances are your team will stop giving you their best – and who can blame them?

WHEN YOU PRAISE PEOPLE, MAKE IT SIMPLE

MANAGE YOURSELF

Being a leader is a tough job because it is always two jobs at once. You have to get your own work done and also be looking out for a team. The higher up the scale we go, the further away from our original job we get. And often no one bothers to train us as to what the new job – leadership – actually entails. Sure, we go on the odd course, and some are very odd (I speak as one who has made LEGO® bridges, done jigsaws that are face down, been on canoeing weekends and all in the name of management training) but we don't specifically train to be leaders. Leadership is something we sort of pick up as we go along. Sure, there are a few good instinctive leaders, but invariably we stumble along picking up the odd hint and clue here and there – it's a very hit and miss operation.

And a lot of what we are taught is fairly obvious. What I'm doing here is giving you the unwritten stuff – the stuff you don't get on those canoeing weekends.

Learn from others' mistakes

A clever person learns from their own mistakes, but a wise person learns from others' mistakes. That's what they say, and any Rules Player with sense* follows this principle. We all make some mistakes, but the fewer you make the better.

It sounds good, doesn't it? However, you can't just have the odd catchy quote up your sleeve. You have to really do this stuff. That means that every time someone near you messes up, you need to know all about it. You'll have to do your detective work subtly mind you. No one wants to be cross-examined by a colleague about where they went wrong, and there's a danger of coming across as smug and self-satisfied and nosy and condescending because it wasn't you that made the mistake, and that is definitely non-Rules behaviour.

So when a colleague gets themselves in hot water, find out what went wrong without getting spotted. One of the best ways to do this is to offer to help them put things right. After all, this isn't a competition, and we don't actually want our team mates to mess up. It's just that if they do it anyway we might as well get some benefit from it. Helping them remedy things can be a great way of finding out exactly what happened.

Once you've found out just what went wrong, work out how and why it happened. Then be brutally honest with yourself about whether you could have made the same mistake. Have you ever been in a hurry and failed to double-check the paperwork? Or forgotten to check your voicemail at the end of the day? Or negotiated on the basis of figures you took as read but could actually have been inaccurate? Or written down the wrong delivery date in your diary?

---

* So that's all of them then

If so, you need to devise some kind of system now to make sure it can't happen in future; otherwise it's only a matter of time before you make the same mistake. And remember, if you've already witnessed your colleague getting it wrong, you'll look even worse when it subsequently happens to you.

Over time, you'll find that a thorough and enquiring attitude to other people's mistakes, rather than a complacent 'It won't happen to me' approach, will more than pay off. And the fewer mistakes you make, the more you'll impress the boss. It's as simple as that.

EVERY TIME SOMEONE NEAR YOU MESSES UP, YOU NEED TO KNOW ALL ABOUT IT

Enjoy what you are doing

If you're not enjoying yourself, what are you doing? If there is no entertainment value in your work then there really is no point in doing it – you can probably get enough in unemployment benefit to survive. I think there are an awful lot of people out there who really do enjoy working but are frightened to say so in case they get accused of being workaholics or sad or something.

There is no shame in saying you enjoy your work. There seems to be some kudos in being miserable at work, in moaning about your situation. There is a sort of office pecking order where people try to outdo each other in moaning about how much they hate their work.

Not for you there's not. The Rules Player enjoys work and makes sure people know that. Once you acknowledge that work is fun – and for you it is even more fun than for anyone else – you will find your step lightens, your stress levels decrease and your whole demeanour lightens. By admitting work is fun, you are trading in a secret bit of knowledge that only really successful people usually have. So if you want to be a successful leader, engrave it on your heart. Work is fun.

Having a good time at work and realising work is good fun isn't the same thing. Work being good fun means you take pride in what you do, enjoy the challenge and look forward to each day with optimism and enthusiasm. Having a good time at work means not achieving much, talking a lot, ignoring your team, winding up colleagues and drinking champagne all afternoon. There is a difference, I'm sure you will agree. Having a good time at work is a temporary thing. It lasts while the fun lasts but quickly flags once the excitement, the elation, has worn off.

Work being good fun means enjoying the negotiating, the hiring and firing, the day-to-day challenges, the stresses and disappointments, the uncertain future, the testing of one's mettle and the new learning curves. A surprising number of people die within a year of retirement – this suggests that work is more important to our existence than we think.

If you ain't enjoying all this and appreciating that it is enjoyable then you are doomed to be one of the moaners, one of life's victims.

THERE IS NO SHAME IN SAYING YOU ENJOY YOUR WORK

Be passionate but don't kill yourself

I hope you're very passionate about your job. Whether your job satisfaction comes from the people you work with, the sense of achievement, a deep belief in what you're doing, the recognition you get, the money you earn or anything else – I hope you get enough out of the job to feel very passionate about doing it.

But don't fall into the trap of thinking that if you're passionate you have to work long hours and jump through countless hoops to prove it. Being passionate isn't the same thing as staying late at the office. If you have a positive sense of belief in your work, and an enthusiasm for it, that will shine through. Your boss will recognise your leadership skills and, I trust, appreciate them, regardless of the hours you put in.

It isn't necessary to work yourself into the ground in order to be passionate about your work. In fact, it's hard to sustain your love of a job that is slowly draining all your energy. It's what you achieve that counts, not how long it takes you to achieve it. You might argue that if you're really passionate you should be able to achieve the same as other people in a fraction of the time. OK that may not mean you can go home by mid-afternoon, but it does mean that your passion will keep your output high even if you knock off at 5.30 like everyone else.

Being passionate about your work, which is generally regarded as being a Good Thing, is about caring whether you do a good job. It's not about how you work – it's about how you feel. So not only do you not have to work long hours to prove your passion, but it wouldn't prove it anyway because it's quite possible to work 16 hours a day and still not care about what you do. It would be a pretty miserable life, granted, but I've known people do it.

So cultivate a positive enthusiasm about your work. If you don't feel passionate about it, look for a new way to view it that makes you care, or work out what would generate that kind of passion in you, and then create it in your work. Now, I'm not saying it's easy. For some people it's a lifelong search. But I'll promise you one thing – if you're not even looking, you'll never find it.

IT'S NOT ABOUT HOW YOU WORK – IT'S ABOUT HOW YOU FEEL

Manage your energy

Have you heard of time management? Of course you have. Everyone has. I hope you're good at it and doing everything you can to improve. There's always scope to manage our time better, and the more effectively you work, the more you will achieve and the more time you'll have left over for yourself as well.

What gets less well promoted is the need to manage your energy. I don't know why this is, since your energy is one of your most essential resources and it doesn't look after itself. A strong leader needs to bring plenty of energy to their work, and it's your job to make sure that energy is there when it's needed.

In part this means looking after your physical energy. Make sure you stay fit and healthy, and don't wear yourself out when you have work the next day. Just as we make the kids go to bed on time when it's school tomorrow, so you should make sure you don't stay up late, overeat, get drunk, wear yourself out, skip breakfast or otherwise reduce your potential at work.

And don't forget your mental energy. What time of day do you work best? On a full stomach or just a comfortable one with no hunger pains? What environment makes you most effective at work – quiet, busy, pressured, noisy, companionable? We're all different and you may not have total control over your working day, but you can make sure those tasks that need concentration get allocated to times when you're best able to concentrate and so on.

And there's emotional energy too. If things are going badly in your home life, you need to find ways to bolster your emotional mood before you get to work in the morning so your job isn't affected (there's more on this in Rule 47). If you're under emotional pressure at work, again, you'll need to come up with constructive ways to keep your energy levels up – go for a run at lunchtime, tackle the person who's bugging you, talk to your boss about your worries.

Finally, your spiritual side needs room to stretch in order to feel energised. For some people this can happen outside work, while others need to be doing a job that gives them a strong sense of moral worth. Only you know where you stand on this, but make sure that your job isn't cramping your spiritual energy, or in the end both you and the job will suffer.

IT'S YOUR JOB TO MAKE SURE THAT ENERGY IS THERE WHEN IT'S NEEDED

Be a good listener

I don't mean you should provide a nice padded shoulder for all and sundry to come and cry on. In fact, that probably isn't good listening but therapy. A good listener is someone who makes the speaker know that they are listening. As a leader, your team need to understand instinctively that you are someone who listens to them when they need you to. You demonstrate this by:

- making encouraging noises – 'Hmmm, go on, yes, I'm listening'
- displaying appropriate body language – head tilted to one side, eyes open and looking at the person speaking, not yawning or fiddling with your watch
- repeating back some bits to make sure they know you've taken them in – 'On Friday at 3, yes, I've got that'
- getting them to repeat things you haven't heard or understood – 'Can you repeat that bit about Peterborough? I'm not sure I was taking that in'
- asking questions – 'So the move to Gloucester will not happen now?'
- taking notes – write stuff down as they speak

Now why would you want to be a good listener? I said, now why would you want to be a good listener? Easy. You get:

- more facts
- a better understanding of what you are supposed to be doing
- a better grasp of what is going on around you
- seen as sympathetic and considerate

- seen as intelligent and alert
- seen as someone on top of their job

If you don't listen, you don't know. If you are going to listen make sure they know you are. Easy.

Good listening is a skill, a special talent, that you will have to practise and learn. It doesn't happen overnight and it isn't automatic. You have to think about it and catch yourself when you aren't listening and turn it on then.

> GOOD LISTENING IS A SKILL, A SPECIAL TALENT, THAT YOU WILL HAVE TO PRACTISE AND LEARN

Understand the herd mentality

People like to form nice safe little groups – family, friends, work colleagues, town, country, nation, regiment – and will fight quite fiercely to protect these groups. If you threaten them – or, and this is important, are *thought* to threaten them – they won't like it. So don't. Understand that this herd mentality is important and that to blend in is important.

Suppose your herd is a pride of lions. Yes, you can roll in the dust, roar, eat zebras and be very fierce and you will blend in – you will be a lion. This doesn't mean you have to capitulate though or be weak. In every pride there is a top dog – a senior lion. You can blend in but still stand out by being in charge, being a pack leader, being the head honcho.

Blending in is about being a chameleon not a wimp. Just because I say you ought to blend in doesn't mean you have to give up your identity or become a clone or lose all sense of your individuality. All you have to do is know and understand herd mentality – and then use it to your own advantage. I once saw an employee reduced to tears because he didn't know the system, and the herd – his fellow workers – turned on him. He was 'different' and they smelled his fear and went for him.

What you are going to be is the proverbial wolf in sheep's clothing. If the sheep accept you, then you can do pretty much what you want with them. If they detect any whiff of wolfishness, they start to get very unsettled.

Study any group of people and you will see conformity. They all like to be sheep. It makes them feel:

- secure
- comfortable
- safe
- protected

All their thinking has been done for them and they can just eat grass, cosy and safe in the knowledge that they will be taken care of. You don't need these things – they're for the sheep. You are the wolf. Think independent, wolfish thoughts.

> **THINK INDEPENDENT, WOLFISH THOUGHTS**

Don't take sides

If you take sides, then you are part of the argument, the fight, the dispute, the disagreement. You have to remain totally objective and firmly in the middle. Stay on the fence whatever you do, because if you don't, then one side will blame you along with the person they were arguing with originally. Whatever the case up for discussion *you* need to:

- take a long-term view
- see it from the company's point of view
- remain impartial
- remain calm
- be the diplomat
- not take sides
- stay independent

The more detached you appear to be, the more of a leader you will come across. If you jump in with your boots on and take sides, you run the risk of making an enemy as well as being seen as hot headed.

The difficulty is when a friend is embroiled in a row with another less close colleague. Your friend will invariably turn to you and try to drag you in, 'Oh, for God's sake, tell her I'm right, will you, Rich?'

You can't afford to be dragged in. You will have to hold your hands up defensively and say, 'Don't involve me. If you two can't sort this out sensibly and without arguing I will send you both to your room'. Here you have:

- made a joke of it thus lessening the tension
- reinforced the fact that you are senior to both of them
- remained uninvolved
- not taken sides

STAY ON THE FENCE WHATEVER YOU DO, BECAUSE IF YOU DON'T, THEN ONE SIDE WILL BLAME YOU ALONG WITH THE PERSON THEY WERE ARGUING WITH ORIGINALLY

Never lose your temper

I don't care how annoying Mo in marketing can be, or how riled you get when Rosa from R & D takes the mickey, or how high your blood pressure rises when accounts cock it up yet again – you will not ever, under any circumstances, lose your rag. That's it. There are no exceptions. No small breaches. No thin end of any wedges. You will not lose your temper.

Unless, of course, it is entirely staged, for effect. Then you are allowed to do it. But you have to be very careful that you have chosen the right moment, the right occasion and the right person for an audience.

But if it ain't staged then you don't do it. And I don't care how angry they make you or how annoying they can be or how justified you think you are. Loss of temper means loss of control. And the one thing a Rules leader has is control.

So how do you sit on your hands? How do you learn how to be calm and well behaved? Easy. Raise your eyes to the heavens. No, seriously. You only lose your temper if you are involved, if you care, if you are part of the problem. If you shift your focus to higher issues – the old good of the company again – it becomes easier to see whatever it is that is annoying you in a new light.

Another method is to simply leave the office or meeting or whatever. Just say, 'I find this situation intolerable'. And then leave. It creates quite a shock and usually does the trick.

Or try counting to 10 while you sit on your hands.

Not losing your temper doesn't mean not expressing emotion. You are entitled to say, 'I find it extremely annoying when you eat all the chocolate biscuits/lose the invoices/upset another major customer/park in the MD's parking space/steal the petty cash' – whatever it is that drives you nuts.

It is OK to refuse to give in to emotional blackmail or bullying or over-assertive behaviour or whingeing. It is not OK to bottle up stuff. Say immediately when you feel aggrieved, so that you defuse the situation at once. Don't let things build up a head of steam or you may well blow. Let it out bit by bit and it shouldn't ever come to a head.

> **SAY IMMEDIATELY WHEN YOU FEEL AGGRIEVED, SO THAT YOU DEFUSE THE SITUATION AT ONCE**

RULE 46

Know the mission statement – and understand it

In the good old days, a company's mission statement was probably: 'Make as much money as possible and keep the shareholders off our back'. Not any more it ain't. A mission statement is now much more complex. If you want to be a successful leader in your organisation, you have to know and understand the mission statement – and then milk it for all you are worth. Quoting the mission statement earns you brownie points if you make sure it looks as if you are really on the side of the company. If your boss doesn't support the mission statement, or considers such things as rubbish and not worth bothering with, then keep quiet about mission statements.

Understanding a mission statement is usually quite easy – Walt Disney, for example, promises to give inspiration, entertainment and information for all. Walmart pledges to save people money so they can live better – but to really understand these statements, you have to read all the small print. For instance, Walmart's promise is quite simple, but there is a whole lot more because they also list corporate values such as sustainability, community and so on.

If you can't find something to milk here – assuming you work for Walmart – you aren't worthy of calling yourself a Rules Player. Imagine what fun you could have with some of these.

Imagine what power you would wield at meetings just quoting some of this. Someone suggests an idea you don't like, you could just say it isn't community-focused. Brilliant. It's like being part of the Spanish Inquisition – our chief weapons are … Amongst our many weapons are such diverse …

Some historical mission statements were very grand and could have safely been milked for all they were worth:

- Ford (early 1900s) – Ford will democratise the automobile
- Sony (early 1950s) – to become the company most known for changing the worldwide poor-quality image of Japanese products
- Boeing (1950) – to become the dominant player in commercial aircraft and bring the world into the jet age
- Walmart (1990) – to become a $125 billion company by the year 2000

> QUOTING THE MISSION STATEMENT EARNS YOU BROWNIE POINTS IF YOU MAKE SURE IT LOOKS AS IF YOU ARE REALLY ON THE SIDE OF THE COMPANY

MANAGE YOUR RELATIONSHIPS

You can manage yourself supremely well now – good for you. But you're not operating in a void. You're surrounded by people, whether they're in the same building as you or not, who you have to interact with. Your own team of course, and also your colleagues, your bosses, your customers and clients. You're a leader, so you have responsibilities – you're responsible for how you come across, for the example you set, for the relationships you're a part of, for the impression you give of your organisation.

And you have a responsibility to yourself. You worked hard to get here, and you need to live up to the role you've created for yourself. You need to act like a natural leader at all times and with everyone you encounter when you're at work. I hope you'll have been practising many of these Rules since before you ever took on the mantle, and you need to make sure you have them all firmly established before you go any further.

Keep your home life at home

When you go to work, you're supposed to be focused on work, to get on with your job. If you spend your time focused on what goes on at home, people will assume you're not really committed to your job. And they'll probably be right, if the truth be told.

Think of the people you've worked with in the past – or indeed now – who spent their time nattering about their families, relating details of their social life, complaining about their mother, fantasising about their holidays, discussing the latest football match, whingeing about the traffic, telling you about their plans for Christmas. How many of them would you describe as passionate and committed to their work? Probably none of them.

You don't have to keep your personal life so private that your team don't even know that you have kids, or that your mother is in hospital, or that you enjoy fishing. But you do have to keep your personal life well in the background, and concentrate on your job during working hours. That will ensure that you do the best job you can in the quickest time and the most effective way. That will ensure that your boss, and your boss's boss, see you as a focused and enthusiastic leader. And that will ensure that you enjoy the job more and find it more satisfying – no one can enjoy themselves fully when their mind is elsewhere.

Your colleagues and your team don't need to know about your personal problems. Sure, you need to have an outlet and good friends to talk to, but not during working hours. If you have good friends among your co-workers, have a drink after work to discuss your problems.

Listen, everyone has an ailing parent, or a child who's going through a tricky patch at school, or an irritating neighbour, or a mortgage they can barely afford, or a sister-in-law from hell coming to stay for the weekend. They don't need to hear about your problems. Sorry, but that's the way it is. I'm not unsympathetic, but this isn't the time or the place for it.

Of course, I realise that there are occasionally major problems that will have some impact on your work. One of those very rare and exceptional events like a divorce or a bereavement. In these cases, of course, you won't be able to hide it at work, and you should let people know why you're not quite so on the ball for a few days or weeks. But if you're doing your best, and you have a reputation for being work-focused and keeping your personal life out of the job, the people around you will be so much more understanding and sympathetic when you really need them to be.

> NO ONE CAN ENJOY THEMSELVES FULLY WHEN THEIR MIND IS ELSEWHERE

No touching – except for handshakes

There's no need to touch the people you work with and there may be several reasons not to. As with so many Rules, it makes your life much simpler if you just apply the same Rule to everything – unless you're shaking hands, there should be no physical contact.

This gives you an air of detachment, separateness, autonomy that suits your position as a Rules Player. You are apart from the crowd. Friendly but not over-friendly. Your colleagues and team members may not consciously realise why you seem to stand apart, but the no touching Rule is part of it.

On top of that, if you don't touch people, you can't touch them inappropriately. Yes, I know you have no intention of doing that, but do they define 'inappropriately' the same way you do? Where do they stand on an arm round the shoulder, a hand in the small of the back, a soft punch on the arm, a congratulatory hug? Every customer and every colleague will be slightly different here, so how are you going to assess and keep track of them all? So much easier just never to touch them.

Every touch is different too. Even if it's not interpreted as inappropriate it could still be seen as patronising, or even creepy. Look, it doesn't matter if you and they are male or female, straight or LGBTQ+, young or old, senior or junior – it's a minefield and you don't want to have to pick your way through it. So do yourself a favour and don't.

Of course a handshake is different. It can be rude not to shake hands. By all means come up with a personal style of handshake (two hands, for example) but don't clap the other person on the shoulder when you shake hands – that would be overstepping this Rule. If you work in an industry where *literally* everyone high fives you should be the last to adopt the habit, but it is a form of handshake. Just a simple high five mind you, no fancy routines.

And what about staff and colleagues you socialise with outside work? Even Rules Players may have a few of them. What you do outside work with your close friends is your own business, but once you're on company time, and company turf, you stick to this Rule.

IT'S A MINEFIELD AND YOU DON'T WANT TO HAVE TO PICK YOUR WAY THROUGH IT

Don't misuse your authority

Now you're a leader, you have authority. In the eyes of your team, and of everyone around you. You might now be senior to some of your old colleagues, and to you they might just feel like old mates – but they're not. *They* recognise the difference, so you must recognise it too. That doesn't mean you have to start lording it over them, but you need to be aware that, for example, if you ask a favour ('Could you grab me a coffee?') they kinda have to do it now. So it's not actually a favour, is it? That doesn't mean you can't ask, but you must understand that it's no longer a favour, it's now a politely worded instruction.

It has become hard for your subordinates – because that's ultimately what they are – to say no to you. So it's down to you to make sure you don't ask them to do anything that they might be entitled to decline, but feel unable to. If you ask an equal colleague how they feel about working late, they'll let you know if they don't want to. But ask a subordinate the same question, even hypothetically, and they might feel they have to show willing. If you actually want them to work late, you'll have to have a proper, private conversation about it, in which you genuinely discuss whether it works for them, and if so what their parameters would be.

The biggest impact of this Rule is what it means for romantic relationships. Whether you like it or not, there is now a power imbalance between you and your team members, and that makes it impossible for any romance to be on a level footing. However genuine and well-intentioned you are, however uninterested you might be in exercising power in a relationship, the imbalance is there and will affect the other person whether you like it or not. Not to mention the fact that, for them, dating the boss is an invidious position to be in with the rest of the team. Therefore the only acceptable answer is never to have a romantic relationship with anyone who is subordinate to you at work.

If you're wondering how to square this with the fact that so many people meet their life partner in the workplace, that's simple. If this person is absolutely the *one*, they'll be worth giving up the job for, won't they? You're a talented leader, you'll find another job easily. In fact you may be able to move sideways – or better still upwards – within the organisation, into a position where you no longer work together.

> *THEY* RECOGNISE THE DIFFERENCE, SO YOU MUST RECOGNISE IT TOO

Exude confidence and energy

I once had to give a talk to a large group of businesswomen about stress management. As I walked to the front to start my talk, I noticed that there was no lectern for notes (not that I had any anyway), nowhere to stand. There was a desk with a chair behind it. If I sat there I would have been lost to view to anyone who wasn't in the front row and it would have seemed very stilted and formal. I could have stood there with my arms behind my back looking like King Charles talking to the palace staff. I could have stood there with my hands by my side or clasped in front of my groin like an embarrassed schoolboy. But I was about to talk about stress – and its management. I needed to look relaxed, calm – as if I was practising what I was preaching, walking my talk.

I solved it by sitting on the edge of the desk. I could swing my legs, lean back, lean forward, almost lie down if I wanted. I met someone several years later who had been there and she said that she couldn't remember a thing I'd said, but had been impressed by how relaxed I'd seemed – and how when I'd finished talking I sprang up and went off for photos with the local journalist. I don't remember that bit but she said I seemed confident, relaxed but also energetic.

That's what we're aiming for. When you walk through the office first thing in the morning there should be a spring to your step. Let the others crawl in looking hungover or freshly turfed out of bed or exhausted from long hours commuting. You will arrive fresh and energetic, ready for the day's work, which be but a trifle to you to deal with, a mere nothing. Walk briskly rather than slowly – quick means keen, means energy, means awake and lively and ready for the challenges the day will throw your way. Not too quick mind or you'll seem to be in a rush. You need to be smoothly in control – not hurried, not sluggardly, not cowed or beaten. You need to be seen as bright and fresh and alive and enthusiastic.

> **WHEN YOU WALK THROUGH THE OFFICE FIRST THING IN THE MORNING THERE SHOULD BE A SPRING TO YOUR STEP**

Pay attention to personal grooming

Each and every morning you need to check that your personal grooming is in tiptop condition. Details really matter. Looking the part is an integral element of being a convincing and respected leader. Make each day as conscientious as an interview day. Before you leave for work check:

- shoes shined and in good repair
- clothes pressed, clean, new, in good condition – no buttons off, no rips, tears or splits
- you are freshly showered, deodorant in place
- hair clean every day – and well cut and styled on a regular and consistent basis
- men shaved – if you have facial hair check for straggly hairs, crumbs, insects, fluff, mould
- women – if you wear make-up this can be as simple as you want but it must be good, consistent and perfect
- teeth clean and in good repair, breath fresh, tongue clean (no yellow fur)
- nails clean and freshly manicured
- hands clean and no ingrained grime from working on old cars or DIY or gardening – wear thin surgical gloves for all those dirty jobs
- if you smoke/drink a lot of coffee make sure your teeth (or hands for smokers) aren't stained and use mints/chewing gum to avoid dog breath

- nose (and ear) hair tidied up/removed
- if you wear glasses make sure they suit you, are renewed on a yearly basis so that you can see, that they are a perfect fit and that they are in good condition – no cracked lenses or sticking plaster repairs

You don't have to become vain or to keep checking yourself in the mirror. Once you have got it right, relax and enjoy it – that way you will exude the kind of confidence that inspires people. I worked with a woman who would go and clean her teeth after every coffee or sticky bun. Nothing wrong with that except it drew attention to herself and her colleagues thought her strange and obsessive. Her fault was not in cleaning her teeth so often but in making such a song and dance out of it. A little discretion would have been much better.

MAKE EACH DAY AS CONSCIENTIOUS AS AN INTERVIEW DAY

Be cool

At work you should retain your cool at all times and, no matter what, never ever lose your dignity. If there's an office fancy dress do, you can laugh and joke with everyone else, but let them do the dressing up. You remain apart from all that office nonsense. Will this get you a reputation as stand-offish? Arrogant? Self-important? Not if you're a Rules Player, because you'll know the Rules to make sure people admire, like and respect you, without the need to dress up as Elvis or a fairy or whatever the theme is this year. Stay cool at all times. Give generously, support the cause, but leave the red noses for others to wear – at least when you're at work. Remain civilised and sophisticated at all times.

Let's face it, you are there to lead and inspire. That's what they pay you for. You ain't there to make a fool of yourself. Just so long as you do your job – and do it well – the way you do it is up to you. You can choose to get involved in all the social side of the office or you can remain one step removed. This sets you apart from your team and makes it easier for them to look up to you.

None of this means you can't have a laugh and joke with your team, just don't get so friendly or personal that they see you as an equal. It pays to keep a little bit of distance. And you do this by being cool.

If you don't know what cool is, try typing *cool* into your search engine and then, using the Thesaurus option, look for antonyms. You get: *warm, excited, unfashionable*. For warm, think sweaty hands – uncool. For excited, think small child on Christmas Day – cute but uncool. For unfashionable think chunky cardigans – warm and uncool. So we want to be:

- not warm – think not sweaty
- not excited – think not panicked

- not unfashionable – this isn't the same as fashionable but rather a timeless stylishness, which is, of course, completely different

The cool operator is relaxed and in control. In a crisis they don't rush about screaming, but rather implement safety procedures and calmly and smoothly handle the situation. They are cool. They keep their heads and their composure. And invariably these are the people who others will turn to in a difficult situation. You don't want someone who panics; you want someone cool, calm and collected.

REMAIN CIVILISED AND SOPHISTICATED AT ALL TIMES

Don't gossip

'Did you know that at the last company conference Raj, from accounts, was seen coming out of Debbie's, from marketing, bedroom in the early hours of Sunday morning? And that's twice they have been seen in Luigi's at lunchtime and Kathy swears she's seen them holding hands in the lift. Raj is married, you know, and I thought Debbie was engaged. What do you think? Should they be carrying on like this?'

Answer: 'What's this got to do with me?'

Good, it has nothing to do with you, unless Raj happens to be on your team and his work is being affected, or you happen to be Debbie's fiancé. This Rule says that you don't gossip. It doesn't say you don't listen. You may find it interesting and knowing what's going on comes in useful sometimes. But there is one part of this Rule that is really, really simple – don't pass anything on. That's it. Gossip stops with you. If you listen but don't pass it along or offer an opinion, you'll be seen as loyal, and as being above that kind of thing. You don't have to be seen to be disapproving – merely don't pass anything along.

Gossiping is the occupation of idle minds – those who haven't got enough work to do. It is also the domain of workers who have mindless jobs to do – jobs they can do without thinking and thus have to occupy themselves with inane chatter, tittle tattle, rumour, lies and malicious stories. If there's too much of it in your own team, perhaps you need to find more interesting and productive ways for your staff to pass their time.

With most things discretion is the key word. Don't be seen disapproving – just don't do it and keep that to yourself. Over time, people will notice that secrets stop with you, and that in itself will work in your favour. Not only will they respect you, they may also confide in you. You will never abuse these confidences, but if you can make use of them without undermining the person who told you, well, that can sometimes work in your favour too.

THERE IS ONE PART OF THIS RULE THAT IS REALLY, REALLY SIMPLE – DON'T PASS ANYTHING ON

Don't bitch

Yep, life ain't fair. Sometimes colleagues shirk and you end up with extra work; bosses can be ill-prepared for their jobs and as such are incompetent and often inconsistent; there's too much work to do; there are too many stupid systems in place; idiots thwart you at every turn. It's true, life's a bitch.

Now tell me how moaning helps in any one of these scenarios. Tell me how moaning will change one single thing. It won't. It doesn't. Moaning is a time-wasting device invented by sad people who haven't enough work to do. And they're usually the ones standing next to the ones gossiping. They may even be the same ones – chances are they are. And when they've finished having a good moan, they'll have a good gossip.

Moaning is pointless. It is unproductive and achieves nothing. All it does is:

- set a bad example to your team – do you really want them all moaning as well?
- identify you as idle, petty, trivial
- encourage you to turn the corners of your mouth down – not a good look
- waste time
- make you a magnet for other moaners
- get you a reputation as someone who doesn't offer anything productive or helpful
- demotivate you and sets up a vicious circle

So, what are you going to do if you are a habitual moaner? Easy, make sure that whenever you do moan you make yourself find a solution to whatever it is you are moaning about. If you can't see a solution, you aren't allowed to moan. Try that for a few weeks and you'll stop moaning quite naturally.

Bitching about others invariably takes place behind their backs. Next time you feel the need for a good bitch about someone, make yourself go and do it to their face. If they aren't present in the room, don't do it. Simple rule but it works. Once they are there, you'll stop bitching.

You don't want to lead a team of people who bitch and moan, so it's essential that you are seen to be above these things, and that you set an example for how to get through the working day without stooping to these lows. Or how can you expect your team to rise above them? Leadership is about attitude as much as actions.

MOANING IS POINTLESS. IT IS UNPRODUCTIVE AND ACHIEVES NOTHING

RULE 55

Stand up for others

So, you're all sitting round having coffee when the subject of young Megan comes up. Now we all know that Megan is a pain in the backside. She doesn't pull her weight, skives off, steals the pens and paperclips, is rude to the security staff, always offloads as much work onto others as possible, blames others for her mistakes and is generally obnoxious. So everyone has a moan about her behind her back and gets a lot of their anger about her behaviour off their chest. But *you* don't. Oh, the others might but you won't, not from now on. You are now a Rules leader and you stand up for others.

No matter how obnoxious young Megan is, you will always find something nice – and genuine – to say about her. That is your objective – *find something nice to say no matter what*. Not only are you showing your team how a good leader behaves, but they will start to feel uncomfortable moaning about each other when you've set such an example.

Standing up for others, no matter what, gets you a reputation as someone who can always find something nice to say about everybody. Thus, those who you might have moaned about know that you will always be fighting their corner for them. It gets you unwritten loyalty and a sort of guardian angel relationship with the more unpopular members of the team.

This is a strange relationship to have but it works wonders – and you must extend it to your fellow managers as well as your own team. These are the people who will back you in an emergency. They will let you know if someone is trying to stitch you up. They will pull out all the stops for you because they know you care. If you need a favour, they will be the ones to call on. It's amazing how quickly the word will spread that you are a thoroughly nice person – you don't bitch, you don't moan, you stand up for the underdog, you are supportive and can always see at least one good point even in a thoroughly bad apple.

Obviously, you will have to do this in an honest and sincere fashion – it's no good lying or making it up. If you, at first, simply can't find anything positive to say then shut up. But there is always something nice to say – nobody is completely evil or wicked or nasty.

So, back to young Megan. What are you going to say? Well, for a start you could point out that she is always on time. Or she is very good at handling irate customers. Or she has a brilliant sense of humour. Or she's great with technology. Just keep saying 'But she's good because she … '.

> IT GETS YOU UNWRITTEN LOYALTY AND A SORT OF GUARDIAN ANGEL RELATIONSHIP WITH THE MORE UNPOPULAR MEMBERS OF THE TEAM

Compliment people sincerely

The key to this Rule is 'sincerely'. You mustn't use compliments glibly, falsely, shallowly, dishonestly or disingenuously. Compliments must be real, honest, open, guileless and meaningful.

Being the sort of person who gives compliments is quite tricky. You don't want to be seen as a slimeball or creepy – and people who do give compliments can often end up seen like this – but you do want to come over as genuinely warm and friendly.

So how to do this? And why? Well, if you do it affably, it makes people think incredibly well about you – it is good office karma. And your team members will be really chuffed and motivated being complimented by someone they admire and respect as much as you. The best way to do it is by being unsophisticated about it. All you have to do is say: 'That's a really smart outfit', and then ask a question about whatever it is you are complimenting them on. 'So where did you find it?'

- 'I do like the way you handled that customer; how did you feel saying that?'
- 'I must say I liked your report; how is it going down with the board?'

Try to avoid using over-the-top expressions. You don't 'love' their new coat, you merely 'like' it. Remember if you 'love' it, you'll want to marry it and have its babies. Not true of a coat, or a report, or a hairstyle, or the way someone handles a customer.

If you 'like' something, feel free to say so. You can emphasise how much you like something by:

- 'I really like … '
- 'I do like … '
- 'Can I tell you how much I liked … ?'

And it doesn't just have to be 'liked', although it is a very good one to start with:

- 'I was impressed by … '
- 'I thought you did really well … '
- 'The way you did … was very good indeed.'
- 'I did enjoy your presentation. It was really rather exceptional.'

When giving compliments make sure you can't be accused of flirting or coming on to someone – keep it professional and/or work related. I'm sure you don't need telling this.

BEING THE SORT OF PERSON WHO GIVES COMPLIMENTS IS QUITE TRICKY

Be cheerful and positive

If you go into work each morning with a positive vibe, it sets you up as the sort of person to whom stress, troubles and problems are but as water off a duck's back. You thus get a reputation as being someone who is in control, smooth, relaxed, confident and very mature. And all for the sake of a few bars of 'Moon River', whistled as you make your way to your desk.

Be cheerful at all times. So it's raining out there and it's a dark and depressing winter's afternoon. Business is slack, interest rates have just gone up again and your boss is in a foul mood and everyone's keeping their heads down. It's still no reason to lose your smile. So it's a bad day, this too will pass and the sun will come back. Whatever your situation, things will always get better.

Maintaining a cheerful and positive outlook is a trick. At first you don't have to believe it – just do it. Act it. Pretend. But do it. After a little while you'll find it isn't an act, you're not pretending, you genuinely do feel cheerful. It's a trick. You are tricking yourself, no one else. Putting on a smile triggers hormones. These hormones will make you feel better. Once you feel better, you will smile more and thus produce more hormones. All it takes is a few days of smiling when you don't feel like it and you will start a cycle going that will make you feel better all the time.

Once you are seen as someone cheerful and positive, people will want to hang out with you more – there is nothing so attractive as a cheerful person. And how are you going to inspire your team if you seem uninspired and negative yourself? They take their lead from you, remember. So if you want them to be cheerful, you too must be upbeat.

Bring some flowers into work and brighten up the office. Whistle. Smile. Laugh. Never reveal that you feel like the pits inside. It's all too easy when someone says 'How are you?' to reply 'Oh, OK,

I guess, can't complain, mustn't grumble, you know, struggling on'. It's a cliché. It's a habit. Try instead, 'Fine, really good actually, doing OK'. There's a trick for you.

> **SO IT'S A BAD DAY, THIS TOO WILL PASS AND THE SUN WILL COME BACK**

Use 'please' and 'thank you'

You would have thought this one so obvious, so basic and so fundamental that surely it can't be part of the Rules. Sorry, but we all need reminding that saying 'please' and 'thank you' is terribly important. It just doesn't happen enough. People say that they are too busy or too forgetful, or that it should be taken as read that they have said them and they don't need to each and every time. Rubbish. The only reason please and thank you get forgotten is plain old bad manners. If we start ignoring even the basic levels of human decency and politeness then there really is no point to any of us being here. If we aren't civil and civilised enough to thank someone, or to be bothered enough to say 'please', then it really is time to pack it in.

It doesn't matter how many times a day someone brings you a piece of paper – it is 'thank you' every single time without fail or exception. It doesn't matter how many times you have to ask for the same thing – you always say 'please'. If someone does anything for you, no matter how mundane, trivial, repetitive, boring, effortless, you will always say 'thank you'.

You forget one time and you will be labelled as rude, boorish and unpleasant. Make someone's day and don't forget, please. Thank you. I once worked for someone who could get staff to work the graveyard shift, come in on their holidays, work overtime, work their days off, take work home with them, work at weekends and work harder than any other manager could. We all watched her, trying to work out what it was she was doing that we weren't. She was getting loyalty from her team that we weren't. I know you are ahead of me at this stage and have got your hand up with the answer. She said 'please' and 'thank you'.

Yes, happy now? She did indeed. And that simple bit of politeness went a long way. I don't think her team consciously knew she did it. We certainly couldn't spot it for a long time. Most of us reckoned we also said 'please' and 'thank you'. But she said it without fail every single time. And when you say it, mean it. A sincere and warm thank you goes a long way. It is also a very good way to respond to compliments and praise yourself. If someone says you have done something well, don't blush and stammer, 'It was nothing really'. That subtracts from their compliment. Better instead just to say, 'Thank you'. Never use the word 'please' to wheedle or cajole. It is, 'Could you work through this lunchtime, please, as we need extra cover on the phones and I'll make sure you get the time back a bit later this afternoon?' It is not, '*Pleeeeease* can you work, pretty *pleeeease*?'

A SINCERE AND WARM THANK YOU GOES A LONG WAY

Don't swear

I know we all do it. I know you think it's cool. I know we have to be modern and move with the times. But I'm sorry, swearing isn't allowed. You can say what you want when you get home, or in the car on your own. But at work you don't swear. It's a simple Rule but it works because it is a default setting – you don't swear. Now what decisions and choices do you have to make about that? Answer: None. None whatsoever. It is your bottom line. You don't swear, so all the tricky stuff has been taken away from you.

But if swearing is your default setting, you have so many decisions and choices to make, I'm surprised you get any work done at all. For instance, do you:

- swear every time something goes wrong?
- swear over the phone?
- swear in front of board members?
- swear in front of customers?
- swear at customers?
- limit yourself to certain swear words and not use others?
- use religious blasphemy as swear words?
- limit yourself to mild swearing or go for the really offensive?

It's a minefield. It's a nightmare. It really is so much easier to just not bother. This isn't a puritan dictate. It is an efficiency dictate. It saves time and effort and having to think about it if you simply don't do it. Now go away.

YOU CAN SAY WHAT YOU WANT WHEN YOU GET HOME, OR IN THE CAR ON YOUR OWN. BUT AT WORK YOU DON'T SWEAR

Only speak sense

To be a successful leader and keep getting promoted, you have to project the right image – the wise, mature, reliable, cool, sophisticated, trustworthy, experienced business person – and there are times when all the hard work can be devastated, destroyed, by a careless word or unguarded moment. Increasingly people are losing their jobs or being vilified for making inappropriate and ill-considered comments. They didn't think before they opened their mouths or posted on social media, so they didn't 'speak sense'. Apart from these major gaffes, on an everyday level you need to guard your tongue against:

- offensive jokes or remarks that alienate any section of the community
- sexism in any form
- homophobia and transphobia in any form
- patronising people
- arrogance
- loss of temper
- offensive swearing
- bitching, moaning, gossiping
- revealing what you really think of people

If you think carefully before you speak, pause and have a chance to bite your tongue, then the chances are that your delivery will be accurate, your speech edited carefully and you will only speak sense. You thus get a reputation for being wise and mature. People will come to you for advice and guidance because they know you think about what you are going to say and don't just chatter on.

They will trust you. Once trusted you are a natural candidate for promotion and greater success.

Of course, this is all much easier if you genuinely don't want to offend people, if you are not racist, misogynist, ageist, homophobic, transphobic, if you don't consider yourself a better person simply because you are senior at work, if you look for the best and not the worst in people, if you genuinely like people and want to see them succeed.

> **THERE ARE TIMES WHEN ALL THE HARD WORK CAN BE DEVASTATED, DESTROYED, BY A CARELESS WORD OR UNGUARDED MOMENT**

Never get personal

It is their behaviour that is wrong or annoying or detrimental to the department. It is never them. And it is never annoying to you, only to the good of the department. The key way to remember this is a dreadful New Age thing that crept in from American parenting stuff. They say, 'She isn't a naughty girl; she's a good girl who has done a naughty thing'. Yuk. Or how about, 'He is a good boy who has done a bad thing'?

This sets the scene though. It may be a cringy expression, but the sentiment is spot on. It isn't the person, it is their behaviour. You never ever get personal.

You can criticise:

- the way they do their job
- their timekeeping, their attitude
- their motivation
- their communication skills
- their long-term goals
- their focus
- their knowledge of office procedures
- their appreciation of company policy
- their interpersonal skills
- their productivity output

But you can't *ever* say they are a lazy, ignorant, good for nothing, lying, thieving, bitching moron. Oh no. Not ever. They may need re-training, relocating, re-educating, re-directing, re-motivating but never being told exactly what you really, really think of them.

Getting personal will get you sacked at worst and lose you respect at best.

The same goes for your boss. You may know they are useless, incompetent, corrupt and stupid. But can you say so? No. Not even to colleagues. Remember what we said about sticking up for junior members of staff or the underdog or anyone that everyone else is having a go at? Well, your boss is the same. You always stick up for them – no matter what. You do not get personal about them, with them or around them.

GETTING PERSONAL WILL GET YOU SACKED AT WORST AND LOSE YOU RESPECT AT BEST

Know how to handle other people's anger

There will be times when you really annoy other people. In fact, being a Rules Player may get right up their noses even if they haven't a clue what it is you are doing. No one likes a smart arse and you might be seen as one if you cut loose from the herd and start looking good and looking cool. They may have a go. They may like to have a pop at you. How do you defuse their anger?

First you have to understand that there are two types of anger:

- justified anger
- tactical anger

Justified anger is exactly that – justified. You just ran over their foot in your car because you weren't looking. They are quite justifiably pissed off. What do you do? You get out of the car and apologise. Say, and mean, that you are sorry. Don't deny it was your fault. Don't tell them it is nothing and they are making a bit of a fuss and you once had your entire leg ripped off and never even noticed. Don't try and explain why you weren't looking where you were going. Don't try to brush off the whole thing – 'I'd have thought you'd have been pleased to have had your foot run over by a top of the range Aston Martin'. And for God's sake don't laugh.

Justifiable anger needs a result. If you have done something wrong, listen to them – they are angry. You have made them so. Listen to what you have done wrong. And then apologise and find some way to put things right. Show the person that you sympathise – you may not be able to give them what they want but you can still let them know that you appreciate their feelings. Don't brush their feelings aside – they are justified.

Tactical anger is, however, another thing entirely. Tactical anger is used to make you do things you don't want to. People lose their temper to intimidate you. The worst thing you can do is let them get away with it. If you do, they'll keep doing it, to you and to others. You must stop them at once. The way to do this is simply to say, 'I don't like being shouted at/threatened/intimidated/bullied/whatever, and I shall leave if you don't stop/calm down/put your fists down/let go of my throat', whatever.

If they continue then just leave. That's it. Say nothing, just walk out of the room. Do this often enough and they will get the message.

FOR GOD'S SAKE DON'T LAUGH

RISE TO A CHALLENGE

It's not easy being a leader. And to be honest, the best leaders love a challenge and would be frustrated if life was always straightforward. There are long-term scenarios that are a challenge to manage, such as hybrid working, and then there are one-off challenges that you can't anticipate such as team members messing up, or friction within the team.

You need to be ready to address these things, and you need to be confident in how you go about it, to be sure that you resolve any problems rather than compound them. However well things are going, be ready for these predicaments, these conflicts, these pitfalls. You might not know exactly what form they'll take, but you can guarantee that they will come along – they always do – and you'll need to be prepared.

Look, anyone can run a team, a department, a section, even a big organisation, when everything is going smoothly. Especially if they've assembled the right people around them. The real test of your mettle as a leader is in how you cope with adversity, how you operate when times are tough and you're up against it. Or, to look at it another way, this is your chance to shine.

Take the rap

Sorry, but if the team screws up, it is entirely your fault. If the team does well, the credit is all theirs. A good leader will always take the rap. I know it's easy to use your team as an excuse, but it won't wash. You are the leader, the manager, the boss. If it all goes pear-shaped you have to stand up and take the flack.

It is very easy to say, 'We didn't meet our targets because … ' But you have to say, 'I didn't meet my targets because … ' And that 'because' has to be followed by 'I', never 'they'.

It is easy to say, 'We didn't meet our targets because young Brian accidentally upset Client X and they pulled out leaving us short of our sales'. But who put young Brian in charge of such an important client? You. Who organised the sale? You. It has to be you. And your team will die for you if you ask it to, if you take the rap when the going gets tough, believe me. Nothing generates more loyalty than a boss who's prepared to stand up and say, 'I take responsibility'.

But I also know this is a tough one, really tough to do. It takes self-confidence, courage, trust (that you won't get sacked or disciplined) and a certain maturity.

You might think it will go against you, look as if you are incompetent, but on the contrary. If your boss sees you stand up and say, 'We lost the contract and I take responsibility – these are the steps we're taking to make sure it doesn't happen again', they won't see a failure – they will see a future board member.

IT'S EASY TO USE YOUR TEAM AS AN EXCUSE, BUT IT WON'T WASH

Be sensitive to friction

When you are running a team you are dealing with people. And sometimes they take it into their heads to rub each other up the wrong way. Why? Who knows. They just do. They encroach on each other's space, pinch each other's biscuits, take each other's parking spaces. Who starts it? Who knows. Can you let it go on? The hell you can. It has to be nipped in the bud.

You have to be sensitive to friction almost before it begins – and do something about it. There is no point letting it go on for a day longer than it needs to. But to do this you really do need to be on the ball. You have to know your team very well indeed to spot those early warning signs.

If you don't nip it in the bud it will grow into a monster. From tiny nit-picking you'll end up with full-scale war, with the rest of the team taking sides.

What to look out for? Silences when there shouldn't be. Odd complaints: 'God, I wish Clare would stop nattering to me so much'. Grumblings and bitchy gossip. Fierce competitiveness where there doesn't need to be any. Sudden appearance of demarcation lines, such as pot plants to screen desks. Books or computers on desks being used to screen or shield people. People being left out of social invites. People being left out of office humour.

I'm sure you know as much about this as I do and keep your eyes open and your ear to the ground. The secret is stopping it before it gets too bad. Here you have to be diplomat, parent, politician, referee.

You mustn't be seen to be taking sides. You must be seen to be taking swift and resolute action, making it clear that feuding won't be tolerated. Call them in. Reason with them. Separate them. Swap their shifts. Keep them apart. Make them work together as a partnership. There are a whole raft of things you can do, and I'm sure you'll pick the right one at the right time for the right situation.

> **YOU MUSTN'T BE SEEN TO BE TAKING SIDES. YOU MUST BE SEEN TO BE TAKING SWIFT AND RESOLUTE ACTION**

Keep track of everything you do and say

Now why would you want to do this, unless you're up to no good? No, quite the reverse in fact. The better a manager you are, the more information you need to keep. Why? Two reasons.

First, consistency. You need to keep everything because you will need to check back from time to time. The question, 'Now how did I do this before?' will crop up constantly. Your team needs you to be consistent and you can't be that if you don't remember what you did last time.

If Jim won that big contract last time and you gave him a slap-up lunch and then Terri pulls off a similar deal and you take her out for coffee and a bagel, chances are she's not going to be happy and next time won't give you her very best. So write it down and check back. Similarly if you tell Client X that they are getting the same deal as Client Y, and then they discover that's not true, they will probably take their business elsewhere. Be consistent.

Secondly, proof. Being a good leader, a damn good leader, may open you up to jealousy, resentment and distrust. Not everybody is as upfront as you.

If your team is giving you 110 per cent and someone else's is only giving them 60 per cent because they are a poor leader, the chances are they will think you're up to something rather than looking at their own bad management skills. It just might be useful to be able to show where successful projects originated, or that you did everything you said you would.

Decisions have to be taken, memos and texts sent, emails written, meetings minuted and/or recorded, reports presented. Just keep a record of everything. All emails should be saved: this is no big deal because computer storage is so immense these days that if all the emails ever sent were saved it would still only fill a cyber-eggcup.

> **THE BETTER A MANAGER YOU ARE, THE MORE INFORMATION YOU NEED TO KEEP**

RULE 66

Let them make mistakes

There is an old Chinese saying that goes something like this: 'Tell me and I'll remember for an hour; show me and I'll remember for a day; but let me do it and I'll remember for ever'. Fair enough. And if you are going to let people do it then they are going to do it badly at first. They are going to make mistakes. And you are going to let them.

If you are a parent you know the agonising thing you go through with a two-year-old who insists they can pour their own drink – and then proceeds to spill most of it on the table. You stand by with a cloth behind your back because you know that:

- they are going to spill it
- it is you who is going to have to mop it up
- the spilling process is important and you have to let them do it and they will progress to not spilling but only once they have got the spilling out of the way first

As a parent you do that wonderful hovering thing, ready to grab the juice if it is going to spill too much, or grab the cup if it is going over, or even grab the child if they are going to fall off the chair due to such intense concentration.

I'm not saying members of your team are like small children – well, I am actually but don't tell them – but it is imperative you learn to let them do the spilling if they are to progress. Make sure you have your cloth behind your back ready to mop up after them.

And after each spillage you don't tell them off. Instead you offer praise – 'Well done, brilliant job, incredible progress'. Try not to let them see the cloth or the mopping up.

TELL ME AND I'LL REMEMBER FOR AN HOUR; SHOW ME AND I'LL REMEMBER FOR A DAY; BUT LET ME DO IT AND I'LL REMEMBER FOR EVER

Make sure no one feels isolated

There are particular challenges when it comes to leading teams or individuals who work from home all or much of the time. It's easy for them to feel isolated, forgotten, lonely, not part of the team. If you recognise these risks, you can mitigate them. Remember though that things can change quickly so you need to keep monitoring the situation. Working from home – if that's what your remote workers do – can be subject to all sorts of influences you can't see, from sharing space with a partner to noisy building works next door. A remote worker who seemed happy last month might be struggling this month, so don't make assumptions.

While we're avoiding assumptions, here's another one to look out for. Just because one person is happy working from home, it doesn't mean the next person will be. We all have different levels of need for social interaction, reassurance, a sense of team involvement, and some will relish working independently and away from the distractions of the office, while others will hate it. Equally, some people are massively more productive working in their own time and space, while others lose motivation, or are prone to distraction, and their productivity drops.

Here are a few key principles to follow when you have team members who work away from base:

- Communication is doubly important, so make sure they're always in the loop. Speak to them as often as practicable, in preference to putting everything in writing.
- Keep team members connected with each other, through team meetings online, and in-person get togethers when possible, both as a unit and in twos and threes.

- Make an extra point of showing recognition and gratitude, and remember the impact of sharing this with the team.
- Organise in-person meet-ups and events, both work and social. Recognise birthdays amongst the group (make sure you never forget anyone) even if you don't get together physically, and find ways to celebrate national holidays and events collectively.
- Develop an induction programme that integrates new team members effectively despite the challenges of working in isolation.

And one last thing – remember that people can feel isolated without working remotely. I worked in a company where the despatch department were two floors down in the basement, and always felt left out. Sometimes there'd be an impromptu gathering upstairs to celebrate a big sale, for example, and they often got forgotten and left uninvited. There was one director who made a point of visiting them regularly, which made a huge difference to them – I hope this would be you. Even being in the office right at the end of the corridor, or the desk furthest from the coffee machine, can leave some people feeling isolated, so be sensitive to this too.

THINGS CAN CHANGE QUICKLY SO YOU NEED TO KEEP MONITORING THE SITUATION

Hold your team together

It's one thing managing a remote team, but things can get trickier when only some of your team are working away from base, and others are in the workplace routinely – what's known as a hybrid team. If everyone is in work part of the time and away part of the time, the biggest challenge can be to find a way to get them all in the same place at least occasionally, to help cement relationships and reinforce team culture.

Apart from that, you'd think it might simply be a case of managing your in-house team members like any others, and your remote workers as per Rule 67. Certainly those things apply, but you have the added challenge that comes with how each group perceives the other.

The danger that you need to guard against is that the in-house team may feel envious that their off-site colleagues have more freedom, no commute, can knock off on time without being noticed and therefore judged, can tick off household tasks during their breaks, and have a better work/life balance.

Meanwhile, your remote team members may in fact find it harder to switch off at the end of the day, be coping with all the challenges of being isolated that we just looked at, feel they're missing out on being part of the team, worry they'll be overlooked when opportunities come along because they're less visible, feel vulnerable to tech issues because they have no on-the-spot support, and generally feel left out.

All these challenges can be overcome so long as you're aware of them, and sympathetic to how each group feels. You need to be creative about finding solutions, from virtual coffee breaks to buddy systems, face-to-face get-togethers to full team meetings online. Be sure that all opportunities for interesting or career-enhancing projects are available to everyone possible, not just the people in the room with you. Maybe you can give at least some of your in-house team a day a week at home to keep on top of routine admin. Be extra sensitive about points of friction, for example establishing a culture where it's accepted that in-house staff knock off work on time.

The more sensitive you are to the feelings of both groups, the more creative you are about supporting their different challenges, and the more you can help them all to see the other group's perspective, the better. Be open about it and encourage everyone to air their concerns so they can be discussed and resolved. Brushing things under the carpet will stoke resentment. This is a tricky scenario to lead, but I know you're up to it, and all of your team will be grateful.

> YOU NEED TO BE CREATIVE ABOUT FINDING SOLUTIONS

Anticipate threats

Threats come at us from every quarter, every day – redundancy, downsizing, takeovers, vindictive colleagues, irascible bosses, new technology, new systems, new procedures. In fact, entire books are devoted to threats – mostly from change – and how to deal with them. If we can think on our feet, stay out of ruts, be flexible and move fast, roll with the punches and go the distance, we will not only survive change but we shall also be contortionists and athletes of the highest order. Of course, we can't do all that. There will be times when the threat will overtake us and we get squashed. It happens to us all. There is no getting away from the fact that life gets fired at us at point blank range and we rarely if ever get time to duck.

But a threat is always that. Once it becomes a reality, we can deal with it. While it is still a threat, it induces fear but can do no harm. Spotting which threat will turn into a reality is the skill leaders need to perfect. There are many threats and we can't react to all of them. There are fewer realities and we have to react to them.

It helps if we don't see threats as threats, but instead as opportunities. Each threat that becomes a reality is an opportunity to grow and change, adapt and rework our methods and style of leadership. If our attitude is positive we tend to see threats less as a negative thing and more as a positive thing – they bring us the chance to prove ourselves. If we never get challenged, we will never improve.

I was once employed as a manager by a company that was taken over. The new bosses brought in their own managers and three of us were 'downgraded' – demoted in other words. We had no choice – apart from walking out of course. I was, by this time, a committed Rules Player so I saw it as an opportunity to prove to the new bosses that I was good enough to be one of their managers and, three months later, I was back up there.

Of the other two, one eventually walked and one stayed 'downgraded'. They both bitched and moaned and felt the move was derogatory and demeaning and an insult. It probably was, but I didn't need to feel depressed about it. I needed to get back up there – upwards and onwards.

EACH THREAT THAT BECOMES A REALITY IS AN OPPORTUNITY TO GROW AND CHANGE

Keep calm and carry on

No matter how brilliantly you lead your team, every once in a while you'll find yourself in the midst of some kind of crisis. Being the brilliant leader you are, this will not be of your own making, but you'll still have to deal with it. It might be a pandemic, an organisational existential crisis, a shorter term disaster like flood or fire, or the loss of key members of the team just as a big launch or exhibition or event is looming.

The better you are as a leader on the good days, the better you'll cope with this. It will call on your reserves of authority, calm, empathy, clear communication, understanding, creativity – all the qualities you have established and being practising up to now. Quite apart from the demands of resolving the specific challenge facing you – which I can't help you with because I have no idea what it is – you have a team of people in a state of near panic all looking to you to make everything alright.

A huge part of resolving this crisis lies having a full team who are all staying calm and thinking straight. And that's your job. It's a lot easier if you're simply reinforcing your normal everyday culture, if you already have a team who expect to stay calm and think straight. If that's the modus operandi when they hit everyday glitches or problems, this will just be an extension of that.

Remember, your job as leader is to give everyone else what they need and then get out of the way. What you want is a whole team who are steady and focused on resolving the problem together, who are used to being creative and positive-minded, who know their own strengths and each others, and who aren't afraid to put forward suggestions. Now all you have to do is co-ordinate them, and look after them. Where there are conflicting suggestions, you make the decisions – while making sure that everyone feels heard and appreciated of course. You need to know what everyone is doing – the broad sweep, not the picky detail – so you're clear what's happening and in a position to steer the process when necessary.

You're the captain of a ship in a storm. You need to stay on the bridge, while other people report to you about what's happening in the engine room, or on the deck. Armed with that information, you might decide that the people on deck need to ready the lifeboats, but you'll stay on the bridge (where they can find you) while they do it.

Once the storm has passed, you'll do a headcount and check everyone is OK, administer first aid to those who need it, and congratulate the crew on such a smooth and efficient operation. You couldn't have done it without them. Make sure they know it.

> IT'S A LOT EASIER IF YOU'RE SIMPLY REINFORCING YOUR NORMAL EVERYDAY CULTURE

WIELD POWER WISELY

Once you've mastered the essential Rules of leadership, you're ready to learn how to make the most of the power you now hold. We're upping the stakes here, and building up an approach that will set you on an upward career path. These Rules will ensure that other people recognise your authority, listen to what you say, do as you ask. These are the Rules that true leaders understand.

Now hang on a minute – we're Rules Players here. We're not aiming to wield ultimate power over the universe and bend all creatures to our will. We're not even doing this in order to trample on other people and drive ourselves to the top at their expense. The aim here is far more modest – we want to make sure that when we can see what is right or proper or wise to do, we're able to make it happen. We don't want to climb to the top on the backs of other people. We want to climb to the top off our own backs, through effort and merit. We're just making sure that we don't miss out along the way through lack of influence or struggling to get ourselves heard. If you don't understand how power works, how can you use it properly?

Knowledge is power

Everyone comes across with more authority when they think they're right. The trouble is, as you'll have noticed, sometimes people think they're right when they're not. And if you behave as if you have the argument, plan, decision clinched, but in fact other people can see you're not as right as you think, you can come across as a zealot. At best you draw attention to your wrongness.

A friend of mine when I was growing up had a father who was a church minister. One day my friend went into his dad's study to fetch something, and glanced at the sermon his father was working on, which was lying on the desk. He noticed with great amusement (and passed it on to his friends with delight) that at one point his dad had written in the margin, 'Shout here, argument weak'. And that's what happens – if your argument isn't as strong as it might be, you get emotional to get it across.

The really strong people, the ones who come across as powerful, don't need to get emotional because they absolutely know their argument is the most potent. How do they know this? Because they've done their research, checked their facts, established exactly what they need to demonstrate and who they need to convince. They've found out who is likely to oppose them and what their arguments will be, and they've got the responses to refute them. So they can afford to stay calm and let the facts speak for themselves.

Real power looks effortless. Yes, a lot of work goes into it, but if you appear anxious, panicky, emotional, you undermine other people's confidence in your authority. You want to appear so obviously sure of yourself, without any pomposity or arrogance (both signs of underlying lack of confidence), that no one thinks to question what you say.

And where do you get that kind of confidence from? From an absolute certainty that you have all the facts and you know how to respond to any argument that might be levelled against you. The more experience you have, the easier this becomes. My brilliant editor at my publishers just knows when a book idea will work and when it won't. She can give reasons, she's always abreast of current trends and has her finger on the industry's pulse, and there's always an element of instinct born of experience too in something like that. She's been right so many times in the past, that everyone listens to her. She knows and understands far more than most of them do, and they're well aware of it.

You don't have to wait until you've accrued years of experience. Read, listen, network and make sure you know everything everyone else does, and more besides. If you're the only one who has read up about a new bit of legislation and you drop it into a meeting, with some comments about the implications, you immediately become more powerful. If you've heard something on the grapevine that will change a team decision, who has the power? You do.

So get all the facts and information you can, prepare your argument thoroughly, and build your experience so that when you speak, with calm confidence, everyone can see that you're right.

REAL POWER LOOKS EFFORTLESS

Be able to walk away

You know how to haggle, don't you? You make a low offer, they reduce the price a bit, you ask for a better price, they meet you half way – if all goes right. If not, and they turn down your latest offer, you walk away. The idea is that they come running after you and agree to your price. The risk, of course, is that they don't. If you sheepishly go back to the seller, they know that you want the thing more than they need to sell it to you, and they hold all the cards.

The way to make the system work is only to walk away knowing that you really don't want the item enough to pay their price. If they don't come running, you're happy to let it go.

This doesn't apply only to shops and market stalls, of course. It applies to all your business deals too, with customers and suppliers, or giving a pay rise, or agreeing who takes what role at next month's conference. This isn't necessarily such an overt process as haggling at the bazaar – although it can be – but the principle is still the same. If you are prepared to walk away from the deal, you hold the cards. For example, if you'd rather hand in your notice and find another job than go without a pay rise, then do it. Don't threaten, don't throw a tantrum, just do it. If they come after you with a better offer, that's ideal. If they don't, you're still happy.

I hope it's obvious that this only works when you really are prepared to walk away. It's a high-risk strategy if you're not, because what if they're prepared to walk away too, and they just let you go? You have to be sure that you're OK with that outcome. So this is at its most effective when the other person cares more than you do about reaching an agreement. When that happens, they put a huge amount of power in your hands, so make sure you recognise when that is happening. Read the signs from them, know your own mind, and then walk away if you need to.

Of course you're a Rules Player, so you're not going to walk away in a dismissive or arrogant or bullying style. You're just going to quietly and politely let them know that the deal on the table doesn't add up for you but thanks for their time and you're sorry it hasn't worked out. Smile, shake their hand and leave.

The ball is in their court now. And whatever they do is fine with you. Best-case scenario they'll make a new offer that is worth taking. If they don't, that's still fine. You'll find another job, or a new supplier, or pass up on the sale, or stick to your current remit at the conference.

Whatever happens though, you'll find that the control you've exercised in walking away earns you added respect for the future. It's a powerful thing to do, and shows the kind of confidence that people admire.

THIS IS AT ITS MOST EFFECTIVE WHEN THE OTHER PERSON CARES MORE THAN YOU DO

RULE 73

Know who you're dealing with

Do you know where your key suppliers went on holiday last year? Do you know why your colleagues left their last job? Do you know which of your customers have kids? When was the last time one of your bosses messed up badly at work, and why? What irritates your newest team member the most? If you can answer all of those questions, give yourself a gold star.

If you want to impress someone, compete with them, make them happy, clinch a deal with them, you need to know everything you can about them. Not just facts and figures (although those too) but also what makes them tick. What their likes and dislikes are, what scares them, what their weaknesses and strengths are.

Now look, we're Rules Players. We're not collecting dirt on people to use as leverage. We don't blackmail people. It's not about that. It's about understanding them, and getting under their skin. It means you can present your customer with a deal that really works for them, or help your colleague at a key moment, rather than keep offering help they don't need. It means you can produce a report that really catches the boss's eye, or convince your CEO to adopt your proposal.

You can do what you like really, so long as you understand the people you're dealing with. I used to have a colleague whose department was always full of the latest, shiny, state-of-the-art equipment. It meant they could perform at the top of their game and they used to win accolades. I asked him once how come, when his boss was really risk-averse, he had persuaded her to invest the departmental budget in equipment that was untested elsewhere in the company. He informed me conspiratorially that his boss was terrified of being left behind. So whenever he wanted her to upgrade anything, he just impressed on her how dreadful it would be *not* to invest, and to fall gradually behind other departments. In the end he converted her to his way of thinking as their advanced software and equipment served them so well. In other words, he used his knowledge to benefit not only himself but also his company and his boss.

You need to talk to people to understand them, and you need to listen to what they say and pick up on clues. File odd comments away for later use. Ask questions that will establish where their real loyalties, worries, enthusiasm, fears, satisfaction and interests lie.

You're doing this for their benefit as much as for yours. You can give them what they want, once you know what it is. Of course you'll also gain respect and your hit rate for reaching agreements will go up considerably, which will earn you kudos among your colleagues. What's to lose?

YOU'RE DOING THIS FOR THEIR BENEFIT AS MUCH AS FOR YOURS

RULE 74

Be authoritative

People are very suggestible you know. If you look powerful, they'll assume you are powerful – in other words they'll give you power, so their assumption is self-fulfilling. Clearly the other Rules in this book are important too because you don't want to undermine your position. If everything about you comes together as a unified whole, you'll be what you seem, and then you'll achieve real authority.

I remember a job I did when I was about 21. I had to organise people much older and more senior than me, and get their co-operation. One day I was talking to one of them and mentioned my age. He was astounded, and couldn't believe how young I was. He thought I was at least 30. I said, 'Thanks a bunch. Do I really look that old?'.* His reply was, 'Actually, no. It's just that you have such an air of authority I assumed you must be older'. That presumably explained why everyone generally did what I told them, and it taught me a really useful Rule.

So what are the things that make you authoritative? I hear you ask. Well, we've covered some of them already, but in the end it's about giving the impression that you're sure of yourself, and on home ground. Appear confident, however you feel inside. The more you practise this, the more real it becomes, and soon you'll be a truly confident and authoritative person. To begin with you'll feel more confident in your everyday work, and as time goes on and you get more practised at it, you'll feel the same in more challenging situations – meeting customers, talking to management, speaking in public.

So a ready smile, a firm handshake, a confident walk … all the stuff we've looked at before. But emotion comes into it too. Be positive – you're allowed to have bad days, but you're not allowed to let it

---

* Oh for the days when I thought 30 was old …

show. Look, you can't get much more powerful than a monarch, and when did you ever see Queen Elizabeth II on a bad day? No idea, have you? She must have had them, but did she let it show? Of course she didn't. So copy her, and stay positive at all times.

You need a confident voice too, so practise if you need to. Don't talk too fast, and keep your voice strong. The words you use matter as well. Avoid verbal tics such as asking for approval or agreement with 'don't you think?' or 'do you know what I mean?'. Similarly, state facts as facts, don't preface them with 'I think … ' or, worse (in a work situation), 'I feel … '. You don't *think* the facts point to this proposal, you *know* they do. So just say so.

Watch the people around you. Think about which of them has natural authority and which don't, and study them to see what it is that gives that impression. Then reflect that back on yourself and see which habits to drop and which to reinforce. Before you know it, you'll have 'em eating out of your hand.

YOU'RE ALLOWED TO HAVE BAD DAYS, BUT YOU'RE NOT ALLOWED TO LET IT SHOW

Be likeable

It's just so simple. We'd all rather oblige people we like than people we don't. We'd much rather help them out than help out the colleague who's always whingeing or the boss who never bothers to say thank you. We care more about what likeable people think of us – we generally want to be liked by the people who we like – so we're less inclined to fall out with them, and less willing to say no to them. We're more willing to align ourselves with someone popular than someone unpopular.

All of which means that if people like you, they're more inclined to:

- respect you
- agree with you
- do as you ask
- say yes to you
- back you up

In other words, they willingly put more power into your hands. They're more likely to follow your lead than someone they dislike.

Remember, power is a thing to be used wisely, very wisely. We don't take advantage of other people's goodwill. In any case they can generally tell and they'll like us less for it, so it's neither ethical nor even productive. You don't turn on the charm just when you need it, and switch it off again afterwards, because even if you were manipulative enough to do that, which of course you're not, it wouldn't work.

You have to be likeable all the time. You want a long, slow drip feed of likeability so that each time you want someone to help you, you're already on their list of people they want to support. I know that could sound Machiavellian but if you play by the Rules you'll want to treat people as well as you can anyway, so it's just a matter of being the person you want to be.

How to be likeable? That's easy. For a start, you're not putting on an act. Be natural, be yourself, be open, and just switch on some behaviours and switch off others. So what will you switch on? Friendliness, remembering to greet people when you see them, acknowledging other people's contributions, saying thank you, treating everyone equally, showing an interest in them, listening to other people's views, being approachable, being even-tempered. That was easy, wasn't it? All the stuff your mother always told you to do, I hope.

And switch off whingeing, losing your rag, ignoring people junior to you, taking credit for other people's ideas, talking over people, and all the traits you dislike in other people. Now that should all be perfectly achievable, whether you're shy or extrovert, nervous or confident, because these are just behaviours, not personality traits. Anyone can do it.

IF PEOPLE LIKE YOU THEY WILLINGLY PUT MORE POWER INTO YOUR HANDS

Know who you are

I've done a lot of jobs in my time, but underneath it all I've always been a writer. Not a brilliant acclaimed literary author, just someone who loves and is passionate about writing. Not always even someone who was making money from it, or whose writing was seen by anyone else – but that didn't matter. It's just what I always wanted to do for as long as I can remember.

Of course some of the other jobs I've done have been great, and some have been miserable, tedious, unfulfilling. But even when I was doing a job I hated, I always knew that underneath it all I wasn't really a clerk or an accounts manager or whatever it was. Deep down I was still a writer. And because I knew that, it didn't really matter what happened to me in those jobs I didn't enjoy. Those bosses couldn't reach deep inside me and take away my writing spirit. They didn't even know it was there, and they couldn't touch it.

And that gave me power. Because I knew who I was and no one could change me. I wasn't desperate, I wasn't scared, I was me. However bad things got at work, I would go on being me, because the job didn't define me.

Some people are lost without their work. They don't know who they are. That's why so many people die shortly after retirement – they can't cope without the job that gives them a purpose in life, that defines them. You can be passionate about your job without having to become so much a part of it that you can't be separated from it. Knowing who you are outside your work doesn't mean that you're not committed to the job.

You're probably not a writer. You might be a gardener or a classic car collector or a parent or a teacher or a party animal. Whatever you are – and whoever you are – deep down, you need to hold on to that. Even if you love your job there will be bad days at work. But they won't have the power to damage you if your identity is not bound up in what you do. If you can take the job away and still be you, that gives you tremendous strength and power, which other people will recognise even if they don't understand where it comes from.

It's the power that comes from being comfortable in your own skin. It's something that grows as we age for many of us, but it can also disappear over time if we don't keep a firm hold of it.

IF YOU CAN TAKE THE JOB AWAY AND STILL BE YOU, THAT GIVES YOU TREMENDOUS STRENGTH AND POWER

RULE 77

Be great at your job

I once worked on a project that suddenly took off and management wanted to roll it out on a big scale. They recruited several new people to get involved and, as I'd played a key part in the original smaller scale version, they really needed me to give the project continuity and ensure the roll-out went smoothly. It was a contract job, so they had to issue me with a new contract to stay on. It all happened rather suddenly and, by the time they got round to finalising the contract, we were right on the verge of launching.

When I saw the new contract, it became clear they wanted me to stay with the project for the next year. However, I only wanted to work on it for a few months until it was bedded in – I fancied finding a new challenge after that. I told them this, and they told me that a one-year contract was policy and not negotiable. But I knew they couldn't lose me at this crucial stage, because there were aspects of the project that only I understood. So I refused (politely) to sign unless they could change their policy and give me an open-ended contract. And what happened? They did as I asked. They didn't have a choice and they knew it.

We know that no one is ultimately indispensable, but sometimes it looks like it. And the closer you are to being indispensable, the more people have to do what you want because they can't afford to lose your goodwill, your co-operation, your involvement. They need to keep you sweet. Not because you're important, not because you're senior, but simply because you're so good at your job.

So this is one of the Rules of power. Simply by being good at what you do, you accrue power. And the better you are, the more power you gain. This isn't about keeping secrets and not letting others know how you achieve what you do. It's true that those strategies can earn you power, but at too great a cost. You would lose the trust and co-operation of your team and your colleagues; you would become a dark power rather than a shining one. No, you don't need to do that. It's not that complicated.

Look around you and you'll see how the people who are most valued by the company are the ones who get what they need to do the job even better. They're the ones everyone listens to. So just become one of them. Simple.

> **SIMPLY BY BEING GOOD AT WHAT YOU DO, YOU ACCRUE POWER**

RULE 78

Get people on your side

Suppose you want to get a proposal pushed through at work, or you need to fight for your departmental budget, or a colleague is trying to block your team's involvement in a project. You can – and should – put together a strong case and argue it calmly and fluently, in order to achieve your aim. But no matter how persuasive you are, how convincing, how well-researched and put together your argument, there's still only one of you.

What if there were more? It's got to be more effective to have two or three people arguing the case than just one. Hey, why stop there – maybe five or six people, or more. So go and get them. The more people you have backing you up, the more heft you have behind your arguments. It's far easier for management or colleagues to say no to one person than to several.

First, identify the people you need to convince. Who are the ones that others listen to? If you can convince *them*, they'll practically do the rest of the job for you. So target the trendsetters, the people others follow, the idea generators that people respect. These are the ones you want. Not only will they get other people on board for you, but they'll be the ones whose support counts for the most.

It's easy to persuade the weaker or more suggestible members of the team, the ones who will be flattered that you want them on your side, the ones who follow rather than lead. And by all means persuade them round to your way of thinking. Every little helps, and having more people on your side can't hurt. But it's not just a simple numbers game. It's far better to have two influential and well-respected colleagues on your side than a dozen junior colleagues without much clout. Quality over quantity.

Right. You have the key people in your sights. Now you have to follow all the relevant Rules to win them round. Understand what motivates them. Work out why they might want to support your case – don't assume it will be the same reason for all of them. Maybe it will benefit their department, or perhaps themselves personally, or perhaps it will set a useful precedent for them, or move a difficult colleague out of their orbit, or clear the ground for a proposal of their own, or give them an opportunity to shine, or make them look good. Or maybe they have no axe to grind and can simply be convinced that it's a good idea. It's your job to work out why each of them might back you, and then get them to see it, as subtly or as overtly as necessary. Once you've done that, you'll be able to approach the real decision-makers as a collective force, with all the power that brings.

QUALITY OVER QUANTITY

Be controlled

I touched on this earlier, but it's actually a whole Rule by itself. In order to be powerful, to be a driving force, you need to be focused on what you want and how to achieve it. You have to have a clear road to follow. Other people can recognise whether you're committed and convinced of your arguments, or whether you're floundering. And they won't agree with you unless they can see that you believe in what you're saying.

Now, other people's perception of you is vital to getting them on your side. And one of the things that will undermine their confidence in you faster than anything is if you get emotional. This applies at work even more than elsewhere, because disagreements at work are supposed to be rational ones. It's acceptable to say to your partner, 'I don't know why I hate beach holidays, I just do', but at work you're expected to come up with clinical, reasoned facts, examples, costings and projections to support your case.* So there's no room for emotion.

If you become visibly heated, upset, anxious or otherwise emotional when arguing your point, people will assume that (a) this is an argument based on feelings and not facts, and (b) you can't have a very strong case or you'd be more confident. In other words, the more in control you are, the more you can keep your feelings hidden, the more powerful and convincing you will be. I do realise that sometimes you will have a big emotional investment in a work transaction for some reason. No problem. Just don't let it show.

You must have seen other people in meetings getting tetchy and narky with each other. It doesn't look good. It only takes one of them to say, for example, 'I realise I didn't give as explicit a brief as

---

* Yes, of course emotions get involved in work all the time, but there's an unwritten rule that we pretend they don't.

I could have at the start', and they retain far more dignity than they do sparring with their colleague.

If you want to project this confident, controlled, powerful image during arguments and discussions, you'll obviously give yourself a head start if you do the same thing the rest of the time too – when you turn up in the morning, over the coffee machine, when the team is divvying up tasks and generally all day every day. Don't be cold, clinical, robotic – you'll just make yourself unpopular. There's room for letting your emotions show, and sometimes a bit of passion can be very persuasive, but make sure you're controlling the emotion and not the other way around.

And you know how some people can just be prickly – you're never sure if you're going to upset them without realising it? Well, don't be one of them. Be easy going, thick-skinned, cheerful and in control.

> **THEY WON'T AGREE WITH YOU UNLESS THEY CAN SEE THAT YOU BELIEVE IN WHAT YOU'RE SAYING**

Don't give it away

There's no point in following all these Rules and acquiring real power and authority if you're going to give it away once you've got it. And yet it's astounding how many people do just that – if they ever manage to gain it in the first place.

So how do they do it? They ask or expect or allow other people to look after them in some way. They don't take responsibility for themselves and their decisions. It's like letting your mum do your laundry* – you undermine your own authority. If you want to retain power and respect, you have to make your own decisions and stick by them. You must do your work yourself. Obviously a good leader delegates, but there are tasks which shouldn't be delegated. You know what they are. You must admit to your mistakes, no making excuses. You must think for yourself – consult others but don't expect them to do your thinking for you. Stand beside the leaders in your circle, don't follow blindly behind them.

In other words behave like a grown-up. A responsible, strong, authoritative grown-up. Otherwise you'll come across as weak or uncertain or foolish or unreliable or scared, and those are not powerful attributes. However tempting it is to blame someone or something else for your shortcomings, you'll only draw attention to them. Listen, suppose you come into work horribly late, and full of complaints about how it wasn't your fault and you just missed the train by the skin of your teeth and they don't run enough trains in the mornings anyway … you just draw attention to your lateness and sound as if you care too much that everyone knows it wasn't your fault. What they are all thinking, let me tell you, is that if they all got to work on time, you could have done the same if you'd got up five minutes earlier.

---

* Please tell me you don't do that anymore …

So what should you do if you arrive at work late? Acknowledge in your own mind that if you'd allowed more time it wouldn't have happened. Then when you arrive at work, say, 'Sorry I'm late. Right, let's get cracking ... '. See how much more authoritative that sounds? Clearly if you're following the Rules lateness is not going to be a regular thing. Nor are any other mistakes. But when they happen, take responsibility for them and then just get on with your work. If you accept the chores, the blame, the responsibility, the decision-making, they bring the power with them.

BEHAVE LIKE A GROWN-UP

PREPARE FOR THE NEXT LEVEL

If you want to keep moving up to bigger and better things as a leader, you need to make sure that everyone in the organisation sees you as a high-flyer, a natural leader, ready to move on up as soon as there's a place for you. In fact, many of the best leaders don't need to wait for a position to come vacant – very often a new role opens up just so they can fill it. Perhaps your bosses can see you starting to get restless, and they don't want to lose you, so they'll find you a new and challenging role. Or maybe you'll bring them a great new idea and they'll ask you to put together your own project team or department to develop it.

So don't assume you have to wait for promotion in the traditional way, although sometimes that will come along too. The important thing is to make sure that whatever the opportunity for advancement, you're already lined up at the head of the queue, and looking like the obvious choice. Make this easy for your bosses, so as soon as the chance of a more senior role comes up, it doesn't cross their mind to offer it to anyone else.

Big Brother is watching you

You know you're being watched and judged at all times, and that shouldn't be a problem because you'll be behaving impeccably at all times. Won't you? That doesn't just mean being above reproach at work – it means being above reproach any time and anywhere that anyone connected with work can observe you.

You have no idea who can see you on most social media platforms, or who will decide to start following you tomorrow. So every time you post, imagine it's going to be seen by your boss, the MD, your biggest customer, the team member you know is after your job, the colleague who left two years ago and might now be about to head-hunt you… and I can promise even if it's all in your imagination now, it's only a matter of time before one or more of these people really does see what you're posting.

You might be reviewing the movie you saw last night, or posting photos of your new baby, or sharing something you found funny, or expressing your political views, or selling something, or exhorting people to join a campaign you support. Can you be certain that none of these things will cause concern or offence? I hope not, and some of them might even work in your favour – that's great – but run them through your filter first to be sure you'd be happy for anyone at work to see them, now or in the future.

Yes, in the future. Some comments or opinions that might be largely acceptable now, might not be in a few years' time. Look at some of the things other people have been caught out for posting in the past. In most cases, if they'd thought it through at the time they might have reconsidered their post (or even their opinion).

When I've been interviewing for senior or important posts over the last few years, it's been standard practice to check out applicants on social media. Just to make sure there's nothing untoward that would embarrass us if we appointed them. These things can reflect badly on the organisation too, quite apart from the upheaval and expense of having to re-advertise the position. This is becoming ever more widespread, and if you're going to have a social media presence you can't keep it entirely separate from your work. So make sure there's no need.

CAN YOU BE CERTAIN THAT NONE OF THESE THINGS WILL CAUSE CONCERN OR OFFENCE?

Study the promotion system

When you started your career, it was at the lowest level and you gazed upwards at the boss, the manager, the managing director, with reverence and awe. One day, inevitably, you will age, gain experience and ascend to the greatest heights yourself. Either that or maybe start up on your own. And for most people that's about it. Career-wise they meander vaguely upwards, often getting side-tracked and stopping at a level where they seem comfortable, coasting, happy. And that's it. Career over. Game over. Very sad. Unless that's really what you want. And if you're a committed Rules leader, I doubt it.

The Rules Player never meanders or arrives anywhere vaguely. You plan. You know the system and use it. You understand the steps to be taken to get you from A to B and onwards and upwards all the way to Z.

You have to study the promotion system if you are to enter it and profit from it. It is simply no use waiting for something to turn up, or for fate to take a hand and propel you upwards by luck or chance. You have to seize the day and make your own luck. You have to know exactly how to avoid all clichés and elevate yourself within the system.

So, what is the promotion system within your industry? Do you know it? Have you studied it? Study the background of others who have been there before you. If not, chances are you are relying on luck to get you somewhere. This may be fine and it may get you where you want to be but it is unreliable – bit like doing the lottery in the hope it'll make you rich and you can retire. It might happen but it's not likely. Make a promotion chart:

- within your industry look upwards to the most senior leadership position that can be held (or the highest you could possibly expect yourself to aim for, they should really be the same thing – mark this)
- now look at the lowest – mark this
- now plot all the steps in-between
- now mark your own place
- now list the steps needed to get there

You now have your own promotion chart and can cross off each step as you make it.

(The same principle of steps also works if you decide that rather than ascend where you are, you'd like to set up on your own and be entrepreneurial rather than corporate.)

While you are doing this, also list all the skills/experience etc. that you would need for each step to be made successfully. Next to this, you can add what you have to do to acquire these – where you must go, what you have to learn, what you need to study. You can add these back into your long-term plan and your five-year plan.

YOU HAVE TO SEIZE THE DAY AND MAKE YOUR OWN LUCK

Develop a game plan

Developing a game plan is a bit like an actor choosing a part and learning their script. Your game plan has to be who you are going to be. Not many people choose consciously to be a loser but that's where they end up. Don't let it happen to you. And it won't happen, once you seize the initiative and develop a game plan.

Your game plan is a sort of personal mission statement. It is different from setting objectives, which is how to be the person your game plan decides you are.

So who are you going to be? Successful? A failure? Someone who gives up? Someone who picks themselves up, dusts themselves off and starts all over again? A brilliant career strategist? A loser? None of these?

Obviously, you could decide to be ruthless, unpleasant, cruel, vindictive, but we assume you won't – a Rules Player is never any of these. Your game plan should include your qualities as well as what sort of game you want to plan – 'I will be successful and still be a thoroughly nice person'.

Not many people sit down and consciously carry out this exercise. It may seem simple but it is an essential tool to get you to where you want to be. If more people did this, they wouldn't end up as prats, or the office bore, or a gossip, or frighteningly callous in their dealings with their staff. If we all had to sit down and write our game plan – and then live by it – we might all end up as nicer people. There is no bad karma in trying your hardest to be pleasant, co-operative, helpful, friendly, kind and honest in your dealings with others around you. Who would sit down and write, 'I am going to be a complete and utter bastard and stitch up as many people as I can, be disliked by everyone and generally make myself as unpopular as possible'? Yes, no one would write it, but I've worked with quite a few who live by it as a game plan. Yes, they may be successful but how do they sleep at night? How do they live with themselves?

I once worked with a fairly senior manager whose technique was to arrive, walk through the department, bawl out as many people as he could, go to his office, put his feet up with a coffee for half an hour and then walk back again being as nice as pie to everyone. When I questioned him about this, he said, 'It keeps them on their toes. They never know where they are with me'. He was genuinely disliked by everyone, feared by most and commanded zero respect from his peers. Good game plan? No.

> **NOT MANY PEOPLE CHOOSE CONSCIOUSLY TO BE A LOSER BUT THAT'S WHERE THEY END UP**

Know yourself – strengths and weaknesses

If you are going to be a Rules leader you have to be incredibly objective about yourself. A lot of people can't do this; they can't turn the spotlight on themselves objectively enough or brightly enough to see themselves as others see them. And it's not just how others see us; it's also how we see ourselves. We all carry a mental image of ourselves – what we look like and sound like, what makes us tick, how we work – but how realistic is this image? I think I work creatively and eccentrically; others think I am messy and unorganised. Which is true? Which is the reality?

To know your strengths and weaknesses you first have to understand your role – the way you work. I might see being creative as a strength – lots of lovely ideas, no attention to detail, generating new projects rather than seeing them through or actually working on them – surely all these are strengths? Not if I am a Completer Finisher or Implementer they're not; then they are weaknesses. Instead my strengths would be perseverance, diligence, stickability, predictability, conformity, steadfastness, orderliness – yuk, surely these are weaknesses? You have to know your role first before you can make subjective judgements about strengths and weaknesses.

If in doubt, make lists, that's what I always say. Write down what you think are your strengths and weaknesses. Show this list to a close friend who you do not work with. Ask for their objective evaluation. Now show it to someone you can trust who you do work with. Is there a difference in their evaluation of how close to the truth you are? Bet there is quite a difference. This is because the special skills you bring to friendships are quite different from the ones you bring to a work relationship.

This Rule is about knowing your strengths and weaknesses; it isn't necessarily about improving them, eliminating them, working on them, changing them in any way. What we are is what we are and it is what we have to work with. You may well be disorganised, erratic, unpredictable – is this good or bad? It all depends on your role. You may need to change your role to suit your strengths and weaknesses better.

A lot of people think that identifying their strengths and weaknesses means they get to lose the bad stuff and only work with the good stuff. Not true. This isn't therapy. This is the real world. We all have weaknesses. The secret trick is learning to work with them rather than trying to be perfect, which is unrealistic and unproductive.

You might be able to find better uses for your weaknesses – but then they would become strengths, wouldn't they? Think about it.

YOU HAVE TO KNOW YOUR ROLE FIRST BEFORE YOU CAN MAKE SUBJECTIVE JUDGEMENTS ABOUT STRENGTHS AND WEAKNESSES

RULE 85

Dress one step ahead

When I was an assistant manager, I dressed like one. When I wanted to be a manager, I studied what managers wore – and general managers. I opted to dress like a general manager and was duly promoted, thus missing out the manager's position in between assistant and general. There is a style for every job. You may choose the job you want. Now you can choose to dress like that job. Then you will get that job. It is that simple. Just so long as when you get that job you can do that job – don't fly until you can crawl.

I have held many interviews in my time for many different positions to be filled. I have never ceased to be amazed at how people dress for interviews. It's almost as if they don't want the job. I've seen interviewees for senior management positions turn up in a crumpled suit, an un-ironed shirt or blouse, unpolished shoes and un-combed hair. I wouldn't employ them as – here I have to be careful as I don't want to insult any group of workers – ferret catchers.

I've seen interviews, again for senior management posts, where they turned up late, in the wrong place, on the wrong day, with the wrong information and obviously for the wrong job.

I've held interviews for trainees where they turned up in trainers – not quite what I had in mind.

Whatever job you are doing, you must have your eye on the next position up. Haven't you? If you have your eye on that job, you must know who has that job now. Study them. What do they wear? How do they dress? What style, level of smartness? Is there anything you could learn from the way they dress? Can you start copying it now? And when I say copying it I do mean learning to dress like that for real. If it means wearing a smart business suit, then get used to it.

There's nothing worse than starting a new job and starting to wear a new style at the same time. It will be noticed that the collar doesn't fit or the shoes seem too tight or strange, and that the level of smartness is all wrong for you – you're always pulling the hem of your skirt down or straightening that tie which feels so strange to you.

There are jobs where you're expected to wear a three-piece suit, and others where jeans and T-shirts are de rigueur. You still need to study the style of those whose roles you aspire to. Are their T-shirts fresher and newer? Do they wear – or avoid – designer labels? Do their T-shirts have slogans or not? What kind of slogans? This isn't just about suits and shirts and tie-neck blouses. Every organisation has its own culture.

YOU MAY CHOOSE THE JOB YOU WANT. NOW YOU CAN CHOOSE TO DRESS LIKE THAT JOB. THEN YOU WILL GET THAT JOB

Talk one step ahead

How does your boss talk? I assume it is their job you want. If it ain't, whose job is it? Or have I been wasting my time here? Come on, whose job do you want? Let's start with the boss. How does your boss talk?

What do I mean – how do they talk? I'll explain. It isn't their accent or pronunciation – how they sound – but the content, what they say. Lots of managers talk in terms of 'I', whereas your boss will probably use 'we' much more. You might speak from a department's point of view, whereas they will speak on behalf of the company.

The more senior you go the less likely you are to:

- chatter inanely
- gossip
- swear
- talk about last night's TV or any other issues that have no relevance to the work being done – bosses tend to be much more focused and less inclined to waste time
- rabbit on – bosses tend to be more thoughtful and pause before speaking (or at least the good ones do)

We've covered some of this before so, if you are going to talk one step up, you need to be more thoughtful, talk about issues that are relevant, talk in terms of 'we' rather than 'I', be focused and dynamic, consider how you *do* talk, not just what you don't do. Listen to the senior leadership and study what they do.

I guess what you have to do is be the grown-up in the way you talk and what you talk about. You become aloof and slightly withdrawn, mature and responsible, dependable and conscientious.

When I say aloof I do not mean arrogant. I'm sure you will have encountered lots of leaders who make this simple mistake. Arrogance has no place at work. Arrogance is conceit and fake importance. Aloofness is being slightly withdrawn, being detached, being superior by dint of experience, skill and natural ability.

> **BE FOCUSED AND DYNAMIC, KEEP PERSONAL DETAILS TO YOURSELF – BOSSES DON'T CHATTER OR GOSSIP ABOUT THEIR SOCIAL LIVES**

Act one step ahead

So, we've got you dressing one step up and talking one step up; now you have to act one step up. I know, I know, it's all too much, too hard, too difficult. Who said this was going to be easy? Not me, pal, I told you right from the word go that this was going to be hard – harder in fact than just doing the job like normal people. Being a Rules Player takes more effort, requires more attention to detail and is generally more like hard work than hard work. But the results are fantastic. In fact, being a Rules Player automatic-ally qualifies you for promotion – if you can be a Rules Player you deserve to be promoted. It's a sort of self-fulfilling prophecy. Carrying out the Rules requires strength of character, willpower, determination, honesty, courage, experience, great talent, dedication, drive, nerve and charisma – once you've got all these, you'll be promoted anyway.

So, act one step up. Look at the way your boss enters the office. Notice anything? Watch the way they answer the phone, talk to staff, entertain customers, hold their pen, hang up their coat, open their office door, sit down, stand up – anything they do. I bet you'll notice that they move differently from, say, the office junior or the maintenance team or the sales force or the marketing folk or the PR people.

Acting one step up requires you to:

- be more certain of yourself
- be more mature
- be more confident

You have to be languid and suave and sophisticated – no, no, not swaggering or aggressive. A simple exercise – do you have your own office? Do people knock on your door? What do you say? A mild 'Come in, please'? or a one step up 'Come'. The higher you go the less time you have to waste. You get slicker and quicker, sleeker and fitter. You don't have time to waffle or use long expressions – a simple

'Come' is more expedient. You too have to be expedient. That's the secret. Next.

> CARRYING OUT THE RULES REQUIRES STRENGTH OF CHARACTER, WILLPOWER, DETERMINATION, HONESTY, COURAGE, EXPERIENCE, GREAT TALENT, DEDICATION, DRIVE, NERVE AND CHARISMA

Think one step ahead

We talked about being expedient. Thinking one step up is about thinking expediently. You don't have time to waste thinking:

- How will this affect my tea breaks?
- Will this mean I can still have my holidays?
- Will I have to work harder? Longer?
- Will I score any kudos from this?

No, instead you will think:

- Is this better for the department?
- Will the company do well out of this?
- Can we bosses sell this to the workforce?
- Are our customers going to be happy with this?

Get the message? See the point? You will start to think more like a leader and less like a worker. You will see things from the company's point of view and not how it affects your own personal petty little desk footprint:

- see the big picture
- see the entire picture
- picture the picture
- direct the picture
- produce the picture
- stop being an extra

I guess these Rules teach you how to be an individual, how to think for yourself, how to stand on your own two feet. But if you could do all that you wouldn't need these Rules. And if you can't, can these Rules teach you? Yes, of course they can.

YOU WILL START TO THINK MORE LIKE A LEADER AND LESS LIKE A WORKER

Talk of 'we' rather than 'I'

I once worked for a boss who asked who we worked for. We said:

- ourselves
- our families
- our bank managers
- our self-esteem
- our boss
- the management
- the company board of directors
- the customers
- the inland revenue
- the government

He said a polite 'No' to all of these. He explained we worked for the shareholders. That's it. That's who you work for. Now go and buy some of your company's shares. Now you work for yourself. Now you can start to say 'we' and 'us' instead of 'me' and 'I' and that sort of thing.

You are now a shareholder so when you have to talk about company procedure you can think how it will affect us, the shareholders – and not them, the staff (of whom you used to be one, not so very long ago).

If you go to meetings it is so much more grown up (and cool) to talk of 'we' instead of 'I'. 'If we are going to implement this new procedure, we need to appraise the staff's reaction first', instead of 'I think this sucks'.

'We ought to prioritise some time for talking about the exhibition' – instead of 'I'm panicking, this bloody exhibition is only two weeks away and I've done nothing'.

IF YOU GO TO MEETINGS IT IS SO MUCH MORE GROWN UP (AND COOL) TO TALK OF 'WE' INSTEAD OF 'I'

Walk the walk

Now you've got to put the whole package together – you've got to walk the walk. You've got to become whoever and whatever it is you aspire to be. This isn't mimicry but training. If you can't walk the walk, you can't do the job.

Remember though what we said right from the outset – you have to be able to come up with the goods, you must be able to lead, and to lead well. That is the bottom line. If you can't do the job, leave the stage.

These Rules are not for the bullshitters or the poseurs. They are for the really industrious, the talented, the hard working, the naturally gifted, those who are prepared to put in some effort and burn some oil.

Study the job that you aspire to. Who is doing it now? Learn to think of them as the person who is doing your job. How are they handling it? Learn to appraise those who are senior to you in the way that they appraise you. Don't moan or whinge about how your boss does the job – observe instead their mistakes and learn and profit from them. Watch where they go wrong and swear never to make the same mistakes. Watch what they do superbly well and start practising their smart moves now.

If you are going to walk your walk, you have to have the right mannerisms, the right dress code, the right way of speaking, the right way of acting, the right responses and the right attitude. You only get these if you are prepared to put in some time carrying out a four-point plan:

- watching
- learning
- practising
- incorporating

If you are prepared to do these four things, you will fly. Of course, you also have to do these without anyone knowing what you are doing – as well as doing your normal everyday job. Tough order? Of course. Who said it was going to be easy?

> **YOU'VE GOT TO BECOME WHOEVER AND WHATEVER IT IS YOU ASPIRE TO BE**

Address corporate issues and problems

We talked about looking at things from the company's point of view and not from your own. You have to take this further and talk only about corporate issues and problems even when you are talking to yourself or close colleagues. You have to convince them you are already a leader.

I remember doing my first book and naturally being terribly concerned with the look of it – did the cover look right, feel right, smell right? The marketing manager, obviously getting fed up with the interminable dreary phone calls from me to check up on every little detail, finally said, 'Tins of beans, dear boy, tins of beans'. I didn't know what he meant and he had to explain it all in words of one syllable. Each book is a product – a tin of beans – it sits on a shelf and gets bought or not bought depending on factors over which I, the mere little cog writer, have no control – such as the position of the book on the shelves, the competition stationed nearby, the weather, any discounts the bookstore happens to be offering, and on and on and on. All of these things, including fascinating things, such as the colour of the cover, can affect sales. It was my job to supply the text and then to start thinking about the corporate issues, such as how many tins of beans get sold in any accounting period, what my percentage share of any tin of beans is, what the next tin of beans will be, and can we sell them spaghetti next time?

When problems crop up, it is easy to see things from your own point of view – how it directly affects you. Once you make the leap to corporate speak, it gets easier to stop doing this and to start seeing problems from the company's point of view. This doesn't mean you have to become a company person hook, line and sinker. In fact, you are allowed to be honest and express your opinion.

If it stinks it stinks – and you should say so. But say so from the company's point of view and not your own.

If the company suggests a new procedure, immediately think how it affects your customers and not you.

> **IF THE COMPANY SUGGESTS A NEW PROCEDURE, IMMEDIATELY THINK HOW IT AFFECTS YOUR CUSTOMERS AND NOT YOU**

Spend more time with senior staff

No matter what level you are in the company, you can spend time with senior members of staff and they won't even realise it if you handle it right. Draw attention to yourself and you will be spotted as an interloper, a spy, an intruder, a gatecrasher. Remember as a small child you could attend grown-up parties if you stayed quiet. They forgot you were there. Once spotted, you got carried off to bed – where you belonged. It's the same in management. You can hang around and learn, but don't blow it or you'll be sent back to bed metaphorically.

When I was an office junior I noticed that senior members of staff tended to hang back after meetings sort of chewing the fat amongst themselves. The juniors scuttled off leaving these big-wigs to chat. I found that if I hung around also, sort of tidying up the table, emptying ashtrays (those were the days) and keeping quiet, then I got to overhear a lot and was even consulted on the odd occasion – 'Ah, Richard, you're part of the new invoicing procedures, what do you think of them?'. This was my chance to shine. I blew it, of course, and stammered and blushed and was tongue-tied and useless. Next time I got it better and eventually got it right.

There came a time when I was asked something and I was coherent, confident and mature. Strange that I was also whisked up the promotion ladder quite rapidly very soon after. This was when I was working for a very old-fashioned British company and their promotion route was very fixed, you had to follow a very set procedure. I was allowed to bypass this system and I put it all down to hanging around the top guns.

Sometimes you will notice a boss sitting on their own at a lunch or social occasion. Most 'humble workers' are too nervous to go up to them and chat or so entrenched in their social class thing that they can't talk to them. Bugger that. Go up and make small talk. You'll be amazed how often bosses are grateful for a junior talking to them because they too are human and feel isolated, lonely, ignored, forgotten. They are glad of a chat, just so long as you don't take advantage and ask about a pay rise or time off or your holidays. But it is OK to ask about their experiences – 'So how did you get into marketing, Ms Patel?'.

You may well find you pick up useful hints and tips as well as getting ready for the next Rule – getting people to assume you have already made the step.

YOU'LL BE AMAZED HOW OFTEN BOSSES ARE GRATEFUL FOR A JUNIOR TALKING TO THEM

Get people to assume you have already made the step

Act like a leader and people will accept you as one. Act like an office junior and that's what people will think you are. So how are we going to get people to make this assumption?

- Be confident and assertive and sound mature: 'Yes, we can do that – I'll make sure we get on to that immediately'.
- If you come to work wearing trainers and a track suit, you won't command the same respect as you would if you wore a smart business suit and looked the part – or whatever equivalent is appropriate to your industry.
- Don't talk of 'I' and refer every problem back to how it affects you: 'I can't work through my lunch break, I'm entitled to my hour off' – instead say 'We' and see things from the company's point of view, what's best for the whole organisation: 'We need to pull together here, I'm happy to work through the lunch break to help us get this problem solved'.
- Discuss company issues, what your department's plans are for the future, how the change in interest rates is going to affect business over the next few months and what you are going to do about exchange rates.
- Talk about parts of the company that you don't directly work in. If you're in marketing, discuss the challenges facing accounts. If you lead a development team, show an interest in what PR are up to.

Basically, what you have to do is get people to recognise you as a heavyweight and not a lightweight. Be serious, mature, grown up and adult. This doesn't mean you have to be a geek, a nerd, a swot, a goody goody or a bore. You can still take a joke, enjoy a laugh, smile, be lighthearted and jovial, be fun and full of beans. You need to project a mature but fun image. You need to make people aware that you:

- know the job
- are experienced
- are serious
- are reliable and responsible
- are trustworthy
- are in the job you want to be in

So, take to sauntering around the place looking suave and cool and being very stylish and grown up, make the appropriate noises and make sure that when you get offered the job you are after, you can already do it.

BE SERIOUS, MATURE, GROWN UP AND ADULT

Prepare for the step after next

Sorry but you can't coast. You are a Rules Player now and you must stick at it – no days off, no rests, no breaks, no putting your feet up drinking coffee and staring into space. Back to the grindstone. So, you've got your eye on the next step, the next job. Fine, good. But what about after that? What's your next step? What's your next target?

Even before you've got your next promotion you should already be practising for the next step. Because if you aren't getting ready now, when will you be? There is always an opportunity to miss a step out, to skip over a promotion if you play this game well. I'm not suggesting this should always be your aim, but be prepared and positioned just in case it happens.

Of course, you have your long and short-term plans – so you will have plotted your career path and know the steps you have to take on your great journey. Even now you will be getting people to assume you have already made the next step, acting the part of the next step, walking your walk, and talking as if you were already the boss, but it doesn't hurt to start practising for the step after that.

Letting people see that you are officer material is no bad thing. Once people get in the habit of assuming you are a high-flyer, you become one. If you dress down, talk trivia, don't pull your weight and act like you are a drudge or a drone, you will get accepted as that – and stay right where you are.

Look around the office. Can you spot the drudges and the drones? The worker ants? The plodders and the sloggers? Now look again and spot the high-flyers, the heavyweights, the go-getters, the live wires. Can you see the difference? Can you see what you have to do? Can you see how acting the part makes you that part? Can you? Can you?

Whatever step you are preparing for, make sure that everything you do is genuine, real and worthwhile. I once worked with a young man who was a high-flyer. He was preparing for his next step. He took to coming to work carrying a briefcase when none of his colleagues did – none of us needed one. Trouble is Ray's briefcase fell open one day and revealed to the entire world that all it contained was his sandwiches, a newspaper and a set of keys. It was humiliating for him, embarrassing for us and sad for everyone. Make sure your briefcase is full of real stuff just in case this – or anything like it – happens to you.

ONCE PEOPLE GET IN THE HABIT OF ASSUMING YOU ARE A HIGH-FLYER, YOU BECOME ONE

Be well up on new management techniques

You cannot afford ever to stand still, to rest on your laurels, to sit back and take it easy. All the time you are doing any of these things there will be someone stealing a march on you.

You have to move with the times and that means keeping up with the latest leadership styles, the newest buzzwords, the upcoming technology, whatever is executive flavour of the month. To stay top of the tree you have to know what jargon is being talked. It's no good referring to it as personnel when everyone else is talking about HR. You'll look a chump if you are still stuck in logistics when the board are now concentrating on client-focused core business or whatever.

I'm not suggesting you have to use these new techniques but you had better know them to stay ahead of the pack – you may be asked. You can always have fun playing buzzword bingo at meetings – award yourself a point for every new ridiculous buzzword you hear and when you have 10 points leap to your feet and shout, 'Bingo!'. It keeps you awake.

And you'll certainly hear a lot of wonderfully useless expressions – for instance what exactly does Blue Sky mean? As in, 'We shall have to Blue Sky this product'. It might mean, 'Anything goes, be creative and set no boundaries'. It might also mean, 'We're a bunch of jargonists who want to sound cool and with it, but who actually sound rather silly'.

If you use buzzwords, try not to sound silly. You should, of course, know what they all mean. You should also know what all the latest management disciplines are and how they might affect you. Try not to sound out of date when you talk of management techniques. For instance, it was called logistics in my day, but now it is supply chain management – and by the time you are reading this it will be something else I expect.

You should know what the advantages and disadvantages of any of these buzzwords are just in case they crop up and you want to look good. There ought to be a sort of bluffer's guide to management speak, but I don't think there is, so you will have to incorporate it into your game plan and see the big picture because at the end of the day there will be a paradigm shift and the best practice of your core business will be a corporate synergy that will play you out of the loop if you don't take utilise your potential for proximity bias and start reverse mentoring your senior leaders to promote human-centred leadership without having to move your goal posts or go the extra mile while playing hardball.

> **TRY NOT TO SOUND OUT OF DATE WHEN YOU TALK OF MANAGEMENT TECHNIQUES**

Write with authority

Much of business communication happens in writing. Often it's email, or it's typed in some form on a keyboard – whether that's a memo, a report, an itinerary, a research document. And everything you write reveals something about you, whether you like it or not. You might think you're imparting information about the upcoming exhibition stand but you're simultaneously dropping clues about how organised you are, whether you can spell, whether you care about spelling, your confidence in the plans you're outlining, and a million other subliminal messages.

You're a leader, and you're expected to be competent, confident, together. So it's depressing how many leaders undermine their own authority in the way they write. For a start, you often don't know who will ultimately see what you've written. It may get circulated beyond the people you initially share it with. Suppose your spelling is a bit rough around the edges, and it gets circulated to your bosses? They might not care, they might not even notice, but then again they might get the impression of someone careless or slapdash. So if your spelling isn't great, use a spellchecker. For anything significant, get someone who can spell well to run their eye over it for you.*

You also want to sound authoritative when you write. Not bossy, or dictatorial, or pompous. Just self-possessed and confident. There are many phrases and styles that come across as under-assertive and uncertain, especially in writing where there's no tone of voice or body language alongside them to offset it. For example, decades ago when I was just starting out I was advised, by a wise and skilled boss, never to use phrases like 'I believe' or 'I think' before a statement, or it undermines its validity. There's a big difference between 'We can deliver in two weeks' and 'I think we can deliver in two weeks'. You can say 'This is a growing trend' or 'I believe this

* I'm lucky here – I get a whole team of editors and proofreaders. Phew!

is a growing trend'. The readers won't consciously notice this, but they will subliminally pick up a sense of how confident you are. Over time, their view of you in general will be influenced by these verbal tics in your writing.

Another thing to avoid is softening your language in ways that can – over time – build an impression of someone needy or unsure of themselves. Phrases like 'I'm just wondering' or 'is this OK?' or 'sorry to bother you' are examples of this, along with overusing 'please' and 'thank you' – they are often appropriate, but once is enough. Not forgetting one of my personal pet hates: there's nothing authoritative about ending a sentence with multiple exclamation marks!!!

> EVERYTHING YOU WRITE REVEALS SOMETHING ABOUT YOU, WHETHER YOU LIKE IT OR NOT

Learn to write reports

It's an interesting thing that many senior leaders can date the start of their rise to the top back to an influential report that got noticed. Good reports get read, they get passed on, they are recommended to other people, they are looked back over, they are seen by senior leaders and even board members. You can write a report just for your immediate boss, or your project team, but it can reach a much larger audience, and stick around for way longer than its immediate purpose.

So if you want to move up the leadership ladder, one of the best things you can do is to master the skill of writing a really impressive report. There are plenty of books and online guides to doing this, but use your common sense too. Think about what you look for in a report from someone else. Generally clarity, and brevity. No one – least of all board members – wants to read a 30-page report telling then something that could have been encapsulated in three pages. So this is about working smart, not writing a thesis.

The first thing is to spot a relevant topic (you don't have to restrict yourself to reports you've been asked to write). Take it upon yourself to research some pertinent opportunity for your department or organisation, for example. Don't flood your bosses with a report every week – they'll pretty soon stop reading them – so wait until you come up with something genuinely worth reading about.

Now do your research properly. Don't just find the information and data that back up an agenda you want to push. Your report needs to be accurate and balanced. If it isn't, and you're found out this time, all your future reports will lose credibility.

Make your report relevant. Whether you're proposing a new direction, working practice, market, technology – or simply summarising the current situation – your colleagues and bosses need to see instantly why this is something they need to read.

Give your report a cover page with a title, and with your name clearly printed. (You don't want the CEO to forget who produced this brilliant piece of work.) Then summarise it on the next page. After that you can give more detail if necessary, in clear simple terms and with plenty of headings and subheadings to make it easy to grasp. Put any extra data in the appendices, except for maybe one or two key and *simple* charts. Get someone unconnected with your work to read it, to make sure it really is as clear and jargon-free as you think.

THIS IS ABOUT WORKING SMART, NOT WRITING A THESIS

Present like a pro

As I said, many great leaders got their first big break off the back of a really well thought-out and put-together report. Mind you, I do know some successful leaders who don't reminisce about that early report that got them noticed, and that's because they got themselves noticed via the other classic route: a memorable presentation.

Presentations are very similar to reports, except that you say them aloud and in person, rather than delivering them on paper. But they have the same power to reach way beyond your usual circle, and to get noticed and talked about at much higher levels of the organisation. And they are similarly about getting across information, and perhaps persuading the audience to follow a recommended course.

Again, common sense should tell you what makes a good presentation. we've all been bored to tears by too much information, presented badly and in rambling style, or leaving us unsure what the call to action might be. So learn from the best and the worst that you've seen, and train yourself up in how to be among the best.

As with reports, your starting point is to have something to say that is worth listening to. Then you impart that information as clearly and concisely as you can. No one comes away from a presentation complaining that it was too short, so long as it contained what it needed to.

You know those routine presentations you regularly get asked to do? See those as practice for the underlying skills – being slick changing visuals, rehearsing until you know it backwards, signposting what you're going to be saying (you know: 'So that's the situation as it stands. Now I'm going to talk about why it needs to change…'). You don't have to be the world's most charismatic speaker, you simply have to be clear, practised, organised and confident.

Oh, and one more, really important thing. Visuals. *Please* learn to use decent visuals – that will put you head and shoulders above most presenters before you start. The key rules here are firstly, *never* put the words you're saying on a visual. Secondly, a good visual is one that enhances, clarifies or explains what you're saying – if it doesn't do that, don't use it. And finally, no visual at all is completely fine and, indeed, way better than a poor or unhelpful one. But go and find a proper guide to the topic and make sure your visuals impress everyone with their relevance and usefulness.

Once you have all the right ingredients in place – the topic, the structure, the script, the persuasive arguments, the visual aids (if you need them) – just rehearse until you can deliver the thing in your sleep. You don't need clever gimmicks or convoluted language or complicated graphs or a fancy outfit. Just you – equipped with the right information and the ability to put it across clearly and simply.

NO ONE COMES AWAY FROM A PRESENTATION COMPLAINING THAT IT WAS TOO SHORT

Capitalise on the career-enhancing moments

Every now and then there is a break from the routine, the humdrum, the everyday. These moments of intense activity or public limelight are your moments to enhance your career. As we've seen in the last couple of Rules, they can be:

- the selection interview
- your first day
- running a presentation
- running an exhibition
- chairing a key meeting
- being put in charge of staff training
- handling a crisis
- negotiating with the unions
- attending a health and safety committee meeting
- organising the staff function
- being responsible for the visit of a dignitary, celebrity or royalty
- editing the internal newsletter
- dealing with the media
- supervising the office relocation

A lot of people, when first presented with such an option, will be filled with dismay and horror. 'Oh, no', they cry, 'Me? Run the exhibition stand at the NEC this year? Oh Lord, why me?'.

You, on the other hand, know this Rule – this is a career-enhancing moment and you had better take the opportunity to shine. There are no bad jobs, only a bad attitude to jobs.

Always look for ways of making such jobs better, more interesting, slicker, quicker and realise that they are providing you with the wherewithal to shine.

THERE ARE NO BAD JOBS, ONLY A BAD ATTITUDE TO JOBS

Know when to break the Rules

Life doesn't run to a neat and infallible formula. Sometimes the unexpected happens. And the true Rules leader has the confidence, the understanding and the presence of mind to recognise those moments and to break the Rules.

Many excellent and committed Rules Players I meet start out following every Rule slavishly. When you're first setting out, this is a sensible approach. After all, the alternative is complacency and an assurance that 'I can do this stuff', which certainly isn't true. None of us finds every situation effortless. It may be clear what we should do, but that doesn't always mean it's easy. And sometimes we're not even sure which way to go.

So, by all means start out taking each Rule seriously. That's the general idea. However, as you become more comfortable and self-assured as a Rules Player, and begin to develop sound instincts for Rules leadership, you can begin to loosen up. Many of the Rules will become automatic and you'll no longer have to think about them. And once you reach this stage, you'll find that occasionally, just occasionally, one of the Rules really isn't quite appropriate.

It's no good persuading yourself a Rule doesn't fit because you'd much rather not have to follow it. You need to be clear and objective. But when your instincts genuinely tell you to break a Rule, then go for it.

Personally, I find that there's rarely a need to break a Rule. It's not a daily occurrence, or even a weekly one (at least not on purpose – of course, I'm not perfect and I still look back on my day and feel I should have handled some bits of it better). But I do break them occasionally. For example, a Rules Player never deliberately belittles other people in public, but about twice in my life I've encountered people who really needed to be belittled in public to stop them from doing it to others, and I've been happy to oblige.

Look, in the end it's about gut feeling. Follow the Rules until they're so ingrained they become instinct, and then trust your instincts. If you refer back to the Rules from time to time (not only these Rules but others you encounter in life too) to make sure you're not forgetting or misinterpreting them, and you work on the ones you find tricky, you can be confident that in time your instincts will serve you better than any book.

FOLLOW THE RULES UNTIL THEY'RE SO INGRAINED THEY BECOME INSTINCT, AND THEN TRUST YOUR INSTINCTS

These are the Rules

I have spent a lifetime watching, learning and distilling the Rules of how happy and successful people behave. I have observed what it is that these people do, and others do not. Whether it's at work or in their relationships, as parents or managing their money, I can tell you why their lives run more smoothly than other people's.

The Rules aren't orders. You don't *have* to obey them. I'm not telling you how you should live your life. I'm just passing on what I've learnt myself, in the hope you can make use of it. You'll be happier and more successful if you follow the Rules, but it's your call.

Some of these Rules – many of them – are common sense. They're a reminder, not a revelation. But somehow you need see them in black and white to realise that you've wandered off the track. Others may take a bit longer to get your head round. And you might even disagree with a few. That's fine – you're allowed to think for yourself. In fact, it's actively encouraged.

There are several books in the Rules series, to help you make a success of just about every part of your life:

The Rules of Life
The Rules of Wealth
The Rules of Parenting
The Rules of Love
The Rules to Break
The Rules of People
The Rules of Thinking
The Rules of Living Well
The Rules of Everything
The Rules of Success
The Rules of Happiness

Richard Templar

Index